THE ULTIMATE BOOK OF RANDOM FUN FACTS

Over 1000 Interesting Facts And
Trivia Quizzes About History, Science, Sports,
Animals, Space and Anything In Between!

BILL O'NEILL

ISBN: 978-1-64845-123-2

CONTENTS

DON'T FORGET:
TWO FREE BOOKS

GET THEM FOR FREE ON
WWW.TRIVIABILL.COM

INTRODUCTION

Did you know that Henry VIII once challenged the King of France to a wrestling match—and lost?

Speaking of wrestling, did you know that Abraham Lincoln has been inducted into the Wrestling Hall of Fame, and won more than 300 bouts in his lifetime?

And speaking of Abraham Lincoln, for that matter, did you know that in 1876, a gang of graverobbers attempted to steal the President's body from his tomb, with the plan of holding it for ransom for $200,000? Thankfully, the plot was foiled by the Secret Service before those involved could put their nefarious scheme into operation!

If you're the kind of person for whom facts and factoids just like these are a source of endless interest and enjoyment, well— this is the book for you!

This is THE ULTIMATE BOOK OF RANDOM FUN FACTS. Inside, you will find more than 1,000 curious tidbits of information just like those above, alongside dozens of trivia questions and did-you-knows, all specially compiled to help you learn a little something - and a little something random! - All about the world around us.

The facts here are divided into sections, covering everything from the universe and outer space to baseball, movies, kings and queens, and math. And, right at the end of the book, there's a final mixed bag of facts, on anything and everything that did not fit in elsewhere!

So, without further ado, let's get started with our first set of facts dedicated to our extraordinary planet - and the universe in which we're all found!

THE EARTH AND SPACE

1. OUTER SPACE

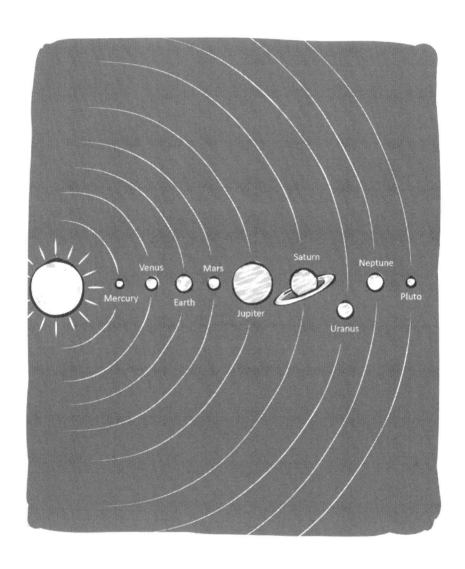

○ It took more than 300,000 years after the Big Bang for the material in the universe to cool sufficiently for atoms to form.

○ The heat from the Big Bang is still warming parts of the universe today.

○ When it was first propounded by early astronomers, one of the earliest names for the Big Bang Theory was the Cosmic Egg Hypothesis.

○ Neutron stars are so dense that one teaspoonful of their matter would weigh more than every person on Earth combined.

○ The Sun loses one billion kilos of matter every single second.

○ A deep space phenomenon called a gamma-ray burst, or GRB, releases more energy in a few seconds than our Sun will in its entire lifetime.

○ Neptune was discovered in 1846, but it takes the planet 165 years to finish a single orbit of the Sun - so it has only completed one entire orbit in all the time we have known about it!

○ There are stars in the universe that we will never be able to see.

○ The Sun accounts for 99% of all the mass in our solar system.

○ On Venus, one year lasts the equivalent of 225 Earth days, but one day lasts 243 Earth days - so a day on Venus is longer than a year!

○ Venus is not alone either… It takes Mercury 88 Earth days to orbit the sun, but the time from sunrise to sunset on the planet is 176 days - so a "day" on Mercury is almost twice as long as a year!

○ You could fit more than one million Earths inside the Sun.

○ Neither the Earth nor the Moon is perfectly spherical. In fact, they are both elongated, like a ball that's been squashed. The technical term for that shape is an "oblate spheroid"!

○ Moonlight is not actually light from the Moon because the Moon itself isn't a light source. In fact, what we call moonlight is sunlight reflected off the Moon, despite the Sun being out of sight!

○ Astronomers have averaged out the color of all the visible light in the universe and found that the universe is - on average - slightly beige. They have called this color "cosmic latte"!

○ Our galaxy, the Milky Way, smells faintly of rum. Scientists know that because there is a cloud at the center of our galaxy comprised of a chemical called "ethyl formate," which as well as giving raspberries their distinctive flavor, has a similar scent to sweet rum!

○ Every year, the Moon drifts further away from the Earth…

○ …while the Earth's rotation is gradually slowing and lengthening our days.

○ Venus is the only planet in our solar system to spin backward, in a clockwise direction. All other planets rotate counterclockwise.

○ There are almost 300 moons orbiting the planets in our solar system…

○ …and more than half of them, 165 in total, orbit Saturn!

○ Although Mercury is the closest planet to the Sun, the atmosphere is Venus is so inhospitable that it is the solar system's hottest planet. Temperatures there are typically around 860°F.

- NASA astronaut's space suits have a tiny patch of Velcro sewn into their helmets so that astronauts can scratch their noses.

- The first food eaten in outer space was a carton of applesauce John Glenn ate on board the Friendship 7 mission in 1962.

- The first soft drink consumed in space, meanwhile, was Coca-Cola.

- And the first song played in space was "Jingle Bells"!

- Neil Armstrong's application to join the Apollo 11 mission to travel to the Moon was submitted a week after submissions were closed. (A friend who worked at NASA broke the rules and added his name to the pile of applicants despite it being late!)

OUTER SPACE - POP QUIZ

1. What is the largest planet in the solar system?

2. Which of these planets does NOT have a moon?

   a. Mercury
   b. Mars
   c. Uranus
   d. Neptune

3. In our solar system, there is a giant asteroid belt between which two neighboring planets?

4. What was the name of the planet that was officially downgraded to a dwarf planet by the International Astronomical Union in 2006?

5. True or False? The universe is constantly expanding outward.

6. An astronomical unit, or AU, is a unit of measurement approximately equal to 93 million miles - the distance from the Earth to…where?

7. Where in the solar system will you find the Sea of Tranquility?

8. Olympus Mons is the highest mountain in the solar system. On what planet is it located?

OUTER SPACE - POP QUIZ - SOLUTIONS

1. Jupiter. At almost 90,000 miles across, Jupiter's diameter is roughly 11 times that of the Earth's. Its mass is so great that the Earth could fit inside Jupiter more than 300 times!

2. A. Mercury. Only two planets in our solar system do not have moons - Mercury and Venus.

3. Mars and Jupiter. There are more than one million 1,093-yard-wide asteroids in the solar system's asteroid belt, as well as innumerable smaller rocks.

4. Pluto. At a 2006 conference in Prague, the IAU voted on two opposite proposals to alter the definition of the word "planet." The first would see the word changed to include not just Pluto in the definition, but two other planet-like objects - Ceres and Charon - that would be added to our list of planets in the solar system as a result. The opposite proposal was to define a planet as an object "large enough to be made rounded by their gravitational orbit around the Sun and to have pushed away nearby planetary objects and debris" - a definition that Pluto did not fit. This second proposal won the vote, and Pluto was downgraded to a dwarf planet as a result!

5. True! The universe was found to be expanding at a rate of 45.5 miles per second per megaparsec. In other words, for every three million light years from the Earth, the universe is expanding by around 45 miles every second!

6. The Sun. The AU is used to quantify distances in space, relative to the Earth's distance from the Sun. The distance to

the Earth's next nearest star, Proxima Centauri, for instance, is about 268,770 AU.

7. On the surface of the Moon. Also known by its Latin name Mare Tranquillitatis, the Sea of Tranquility is one of several large flat open "seas" on the Moon's surface. It was also where Apollo 11 landed on the Moon's surface in 1969.

8. Mars. Olympus Mons is actually a gigantic 13-mile-high volcano, roughly two and a half times the height of Mount Everest!

2. PLANET EARTH

○ The Earth is more than four billion years old.

○ Ours is the fifth-largest planet in our solar system. Only Mars, Venus, and Mercury are smaller.

○ The Earth travels around the Sun at 67,000 miles an hour.

○ The Earth does not sit perfectly upright, but is tilted at an angle of around 23°…

○ … and it is this tilt that points different parts of the Earth slightly closer to the Sun as we travel around it, giving us our seasons!

○ The Earth's diameter - the distance from one side to the other, going straight through the middle — is around 7,900 miles. That is the equivalent of more than 100,000 football pitches!

○ The Earth's longest mountain range can be located underwater. The so-called Mid-Atlantic Ridge is an enormous chain of submarine mountains that runs down the middle of almost the entire Atlantic Ocean.

○ Because a desert is officially defined as an area that receives little to no precipitation, the world's largest desert is actually Antarctica, not the Sahara!

○ There are 300 cubic million miles of water in the Earth's oceans.

○ Because the Earth is not a perfect sphere, the circumference around the equator (24,900 miles) is slightly larger than the circumference around the poles (24,800 miles).

○ The mean average temperature of the entire planet is 59°F.

○ It doesn't take the Earth 365 days to orbit the Sun, but rather around 365¼…

O ... and that extra quarter day (around six hours) is why we need to add an extra day to our calendar every four years!

O The Earth's crust is the thinnest, coldest, and least dense of all the Earth's geological layers. At its thickest point, the crust is no more than around 30 miles thick - while the Earth's outer core is more than 1,400 miles thick!

O The crust is also divided into two sections known as the sial (the lighter, less dense rocks that form the bedrock of the continents) and the sima (the denser rocks, lying under the sial, that form the ocean bed).

O The Earth's largest lake is actually a sea. The Caspian Sea in west central Asia/the far easter of Europe is 1,400,000 sq miles in size - that is more than 40 times the size of Lake Superior.

O The Sahara is the world's largest sandy desert and is growing by around 30 miles every year.

O The world's oldest desert, meanwhile, is the Namib Desert in southern Africa. It has been covered in arid sand for more than 70 million years.

O The Mediterranean Sea used to be a vast empty basin-like depression until the Atlantic Ocean swelled sufficiently to overflow the Straits of Gibraltar and fill it with water. This colossal event - known as the Zanclean Flood - happened more than five million years ago.

O Mount Everest weighs around 350 trillion pounds...

O ...and grows in height by around a quarter of an inch every year!

O Ten of the world's 14 mountains that stand higher than 8,000m (26,247ft) are found in the Himalayas.

- The most volcanic region on the planet is Indonesia. This vast island nation is home to more than 13,000 volcanoes!

- More than half a million gallons of water flow over the edge of Niagara Falls every second.

- The world's tallest uninterrupted waterfall is Angel Falls in Venezuela. The falls themselves stand more than 3,000 feet tall, while the water flowing over them plunges 2,648 feet.

- If it were not classed as a continent, Australia would be the world's largest island…

- … but because it is, the world's largest island is actually Greenland. At 840,000 square miles in size, it is more than twice the size of its closest rival, New Guinea.

PLANET EARTH - POP QUIZ

1. Despite oxygen being the gas required by all human life, nearly 80% of the Earth's atmosphere is actually… what?

2. On what continent is the Great Sandy Desert?

3. In terms of width, compared to the Earth, how big is the Moon?
   a. About one 20th the size of the Earth
   b. About one tenth the size of the Earth
   c. About one quarter the size of the Earth
   d. About three quarters the size of the Earth

4. Aconcagua is the highest mountain on what continent?

5. What is the world's largest ocean?

6. What is the largest island in Europe?

7. What are cirrus, stratus, and cumulus all types of?

8. What major line of the Earth's latitude will you find at approximately 66°N?

PLANET EARTH - POP QUIZ - SOLUTIONS

1. Nitrogen. Although mostly made of nitrogen and oxygen, our air consists of a complex mixture of gases and elements, including far smaller quantities of argon, neon, carbon dioxide, and helium. Depending on the climate, anything up to 3% of the air you breathe can be comprised of water vapor too!

2. Australia. The Great Sandy is the second largest desert in Australia (after the Great Victoria), covering just over 110,000 square miles.

3. C. About one quarter the size of the Earth. The Moon's diameter is roughly equivalent in size to the continental United States, or Europe across from east to west.

4. South America. At 22,800 feet tall, Aconcagua in the Argentinian Andes is not just the highest mountain in South America, but the highest in the entire America, the highest in the southern hemisphere, and the highest mountain outside of Asia!

5. Pacific Ocean. At 63,800,000 square miles, the Pacific covers one-third of the entire surface of the planet!

6. Great Britain. At just over 80,000 square miles, Britain is also the ninth-largest island in the world, and twice as large as Europe's second-largest island, Iceland.

7. Clouds. Cirrus, stratus, and cumulus are the three main classes of clouds, into which almost all other cloud types—of which more than 100 have now been described!—can be categorized.

8. Arctic Circle. The Arctic Circle is the northernmost of the five so-called Great Circles of the Earth: from north to south, they are the Arctic Circle, the Tropic of Cancer, the Equator, the Tropic of Capricorn, and the Antarctic Circle. At 0°, the Equator is the only one of these that is fixed and does not change relative to the tilt of the Earth.

3. ON THE MAP - COUNTRIES & REGIONS OF THE WORLD

- The first country in the world alphabetically is Afghanistan.

- At 6.6 million square miles in size, the world's largest country is Russia...

- ... in fact, Russia alone covers 11% of all the land surface of the Earth!

- Russia, Egypt, Turkey, and Kazakhstan are the only so-called contiguous transcontinental countries in the world - meaning their main landmasses straddle two different continents. Russia, Turkey, and Kazakhstan are all split between Europe and Asia, while Egypt is split between Asia and Africa.

- The world's smallest independent country is the Vatican City. Surrounded by the Italian capital of Rome, it is just 0.19 square miles in area.

- The world's oldest country is said to be Iran. Although the country's borders have changed over the centuries, Iran has remained in place in one form or another for more than 5,000 years!

- The world's oldest republic, meanwhile, is the tiny country of San Marino. It declared its independence from the Roman Empire in 301 CE and has remained in place ever since.

- The Himalayan nation of Bhutan is the world's highest country. Its lowest point is still more than 300 feet above sea level, while the country, as a whole, is so mountainous that its average height is 10,700 feet!

- Only two countries in the world have names beginning with Z, and they border each other: Zambia and Zimbabwe.

- O, Q, and Y are the only letters of the alphabet to begin the names of just one country each, all of which are in the Middle East: Oman, Qatar, and Yemen.

- Almost two-thirds of all the forest areas in the world are in just two countries: Russia and Brazil.

- And there are only three independent countries in the world with no forest cover whatsoever: the Pacific island nation of Nauru, San Marino, and Qatar.

- Both China and Russia share land borders with 14 other countries - including each other!

- There are just 12 independent countries in mainland South America - that is fewer than any other continent…

- … but Brazil is so big, that it shares a land border with ten of them! In fact, the only other South American countries it does NOT share a border with are Ecuador and Chile.

- For decades, the largest country in Africa was Sudan. In 2011, however, the southernmost region of the country broke away to form an independent republic, South Sudan, and Sudan lost its crown as a result! Africa's largest country today is now Algeria.

- One of the world's smallest countries is the island nation of Malta in southern Europe. It is so small and so arid that it has no rivers, no streams, and no large trees, **but temporary waterways can form after heavy rains**.!

- The country of Indonesia comprises more than 17,000 islands.

- Even still, Indonesia is not the country with the most islands in total: Sweden has more than 267,000!

- Monaco is the world's most densely populated country. Its population of 36,000 people is squeezed into just three-quarters of a square mile of territory, meaning the country's average density is 47,000 people per square mile!

○ The world's least densely populated independent country is Mongolia, which has on average just five people per square mile.

○ Spanning more than half the Northern Hemisphere, Canada is the world's second-largest country - yet only around half of 1% of the world's population lives there.

○ Only two countries in the world are home to more than one billion people: China and India...

○ ... and according to the United Nations, the Indian population overtook the Chinese population in April 2023. India approximately 1,441,719,852 – China approximately 1,425,350,114

○ There are more than 40 landlocked countries in the world (meaning that they have no external coastline), including Bolivia, Chad, Afghanistan, and Ethiopia.

○ The world's largest landlocked country is Kazakhstan.

○ There are also two doubly landlocked countries in the world - Liechtenstein and Uzbekistan - meaning that all the countries that all the countries that surround them are themselves landlocked!

ON THE MAP - POP QUIZ

1. If you were to sail due east out of New York, what country would you land in?

    a. France
    b. Portugal
    c. Ireland
    d. Morocco

2. There are only three independent countries in the world whose names begin with F. Name two of them.

3. Portugal shares its only land border with what other European country?

4. What is the southernmost mainland country in North America?

5. What country is also the largest island in the Caribbean Sea?

6. Gambia is a country on what continent?

7. After what is the country of Ecuador named?

8. In what ocean are the island nations of Mauritius, Madagascar, and Sri Lanka located?

ON THE MAP - POP QUIZ - SOLUTIONS

1. B. Portugal. Despite its chilly, snowy winters, New York is relatively far south and at 40° north of the equator, it lies on the same line of latitude as Mediterranean destinations like Majorca in Spain and Lemnos in Greece!

2. Fiji, Finland, France. There are a handful of other states and territories around the world whose names begin with F, but they are not independent and are officially classed as dependencies - among them, French Guiana, and French Polynesia (which are controlled by France), the Falkland Islands (UK), and the Faroe Islands (Denmark).

3. Spain. Of the world's 200 or so independent nations, only 10% share a land border with just one other. As well as Portugal, some other countries in this group are Denmark (which borders only Germany), the UK (Ireland, and vice versa), Canada (the USA), and South Korea (North Korea).

4. Panama. Depending on where the border between the two landmasses is drawn, Panama is both the southernmost North American country and the northernmost South American country!

5. Cuba. At 40,800 square miles, Cuba is more than 10,000 square miles larger than the second-largest Caribbean island, Hispaniola.

6. Africa. At 4,300 square miles - 1,000 square miles smaller than Puerto Rico - Gambia is also Africa's smallest mainland nation.

7. The equator. Ecuador lies directly at 0° latitude.

8. Indian Ocean. Madagascar is the world's largest island nation, and the fourth-largest island in the world after Greenland, New Guinea, and Borneo.

4. CITIES

- There are officially more than 50,000 cities around the world.

- According to the United Nations, 2007 was the year in which the population of the world shifted so that more than 50% of people worldwide lived in cities, not rural areas, for the first time in human history.

- Rome was the first city in the world to attain a population of 1,000,000 people...

- ... and incredibly, historians estimate this landmark was reached more than 2,000 years ago in 133 BCE!

- The first city in the world to be home to more than 5,000,000 people was London in 1900. In fact,...

- ... London was the biggest city in the world until it was overtaken by New York in 1915!

- With a total population of more than 37 million people, the world's most highly populated city is Tokyo.

- Zagreb, Croatia, is the only capital city in the world whose name begins with Z.

- The world's largest French-speaking city isn't Paris - it is Kinshasa, the capital of the Democratic Republic of the Congo in Central Africa.

- Reykjavik, the capital city of Iceland, is the world's northernmost capital city...

- ... while the world's southernmost capital city is Wellington, New Zealand.

- Istanbul in Turkey is popularly said to be the only city in the world to lie on two continents: it is split between Europe and Asia...

- ... but in fact, there are more than a dozen so-called transcontinental cities, it is just that Istanbul is the largest! Others include Oral in Kazakhstan, Port Said in Egypt, and Colón in Panama.

- New York is the most populous city in the United States with approximately 8 million people...

- ..., but it is neither the most populous in North America nor the Americas as a whole. It is beaten into fourth place overall in the Americas by São Paulo, Lima in Peru, and Mexico City.

- There are more than 30 countries around the world whose capital cities are NOT their largest city. Some of them include Australia (Canberra vs. Sydney), the USA Washington DC vs. New York), Canada (Toronto vs. Ottawa), and India (New Delhi vs. Mumbai).

- Delhi and the Indian capital of New Delhi are actually the same city - as New Delhi is a district of the larger city of Delhi.

- Before Tokyo, the capital of Japan was Kyoto. The cities' names are anagrams of each other!

- The capital of Liberia, Monrovia, is named after the US president James Monroe.

- Before London became the capital of England in 1066, the English capital was actually the city of Winchester.

- Belmopan, the capital city of Belize, takes its name from the two rivers that flow through it: the Belize and the Mopan!

- Countries that have moved their capital cities in recent years include Burma (moved from Yangon to Naypyidaw in 2005), Palau (moved from Koror to Ngerulmud in 2006), and Burundi (moved to Gitega from Bujumbura in 2018).

○ In the 200 years from 1820-2020, the capital of Kazakhstan was either moved or renamed eight times.

○ In Irish, Dublin means "black pool." On the opposite side of the Irish Sea from Dublin, on England's west coast, is a town called Blackpool.

○ Ulan Bator, the capital of Mongolia, was originally named Niislel Khureheh when the country declared independence in 1911. Niislel Khureheh literally means "capital of Mongolia"!

○ Indianapolis has more churches per person than any other city. With almost 3,000 in total, that is one church for every 289 people!

○ Paris Syndrome is the name of a genuine medical disorder suffered by tourists who become overwhelmed when visiting the French capital.

CITIES - POP QUIZ

1. Which of these capital cities is, like Venice, not built on dry land but built across a series of interconnected islands?

    a. Moscow
    b. Stockholm
    c. Athens
    d. Buenos Aires

2. What is the largest city on the River Thames?

3. What African country is the only one in the world to have three capital cities: Pretoria, Cape Town, and Bloemfontein?

4. Oddly, the capital city of Denmark is not on the Danish mainland, but a separate capital island. What is its name?

5. What is the southernmost of the five boroughs of New York?

6. What US city is nicknamed "The City of Brotherly Love"?

7. And what UK city - the capital of Scotland - is nicknamed the "Athens of the North"?

8. What European river flows through no less than four different national capital cities: Belgrade, Bratislava, Budapest, and Vienna?

CITIES - POP QUIZ - SOLUTIONS

1. B. Stockholm. In fact, the Swedish capital stretches across 14 different islands in total!

2. London. The Thames is the longest river entirely in England. As well as London, it flows through several major English towns and cities including Oxford, Reading, and Southend.

3. South Africa. Pretoria is the executive capital, Cape Town is the legislative capital, and Bloemfontein is the judicial capital.

4. Copenhagen. The city actually straddles both the islands of Zealand and Amager - and is closer to the mainland of Sweden than Denmark!

5. Staten Island. With a population of just under half a million people, Staten Island is also the least populated and least densely populated of New York's boroughs.

6. Philadelphia. The name itself, in fact, comes from the Greek words "philos," meaning loving, and "adelphos," meaning brother!

7. Edinburgh. The nickname refers to the city's impressive classical architecture.

8. Danube. The Danube actually flows through more national capitals than any other river in the world!

5. WORLD LANGUAGES

○ There are over 7,000 different languages in the world.

○ On average, one world language is lost - when its last native speaker dies - every 40 days.

○ Worldwide, almost 1.5 billion people speak English, either as their mother tongue or as a second language.

○ So, if you are an English speaker, you could comfortably communicate with roughly one in every five people on the planet!

○ The world's most-spoken first language is Mandarin Chinese. It has more than 950 million native speakers...

○ ... which means roughly one-eighth of the entire world speaks Mandarin as their first language!

○ French is an official language in 29 different countries worldwide...

○ ..., but it is only the third most-spoken of Europe's major Romance languages (those descended from Latin), behind Spanish and Portuguese.

○ Papua New Guinea is home to more languages - 840 - than any other country on the planet...

○ ... which means that almost one in eight of all the languages spoken in the world are used in Papua New Guinea!

○ Worldwide, bilingual, or multilingual people outnumber monolinguals - so if you only speak one language fluently, you are in a global minority!

○ The English language is popularly said to have more words than any other language on the planet. Although the total number of English words is impossible to quantify, estimates range from around 300,000 to more than one million!

○ The English alphabet is actually descended via Latin and Greek from the Phoenician alphabet, which emerged on the Mediterranean coast of the Middle East more than 4,000 years ago.

○ Worldwide, more than 100 countries recognize more than one official language.

○ Although Hindi is officially recognized as the main language of India, the country's constitution also recognizes 21 others - including English, Punjabi, Tamil, Sanskrit, and Nepalese.

○ In total, 447 languages are spoken in India.

○ Legally, the United States does not have an official language.

○ There are thought to be around 300 languages spoken in the United States.

○ In fact, there are two times more Italian speakers in the United States than there are people living in Florence...

○ ... and there are more German speakers in the United States than there are people living in Frankfurt!

○ The Basque language, spoken in the Basque country on the north coast of Spain, is known as a language isolate - meaning linguists do not know where it comes from, or what other languages it might be related to. In fact, it is nothing like any of the other languages of Europe!

○ The Native Australasians traveled so far in ancient times that Malagasy, the native language of Madagascar, is more closely related to the languages of Indonesia than mainland Africa.

○ Maltese, the language spoken in the tiny Mediterranean country of Malta, is descended from historical Arabic, but is written in the Latin alphabet.

○ The different varieties of Arabic are so different from one another that speakers in different Arabic-speaking countries would struggle to communicate with one another!

○ Danish, Swedish, and Norwegian, meanwhile, are so similar to one another that the three can almost be used interchangeably. According to some estimates, 80% of Danish and Norwegian, in particular, are said to be mutually intelligible.

○ The Turkish language used to be written using the Arabic alphabet, but in 1928 the language switched over the ABCs of the Roman alphabet and has been written that way ever since!

○ In 2011, the Busuu language of Cameroon in West Africa was spoken fluently by just eight people.

WORLD LANGUAGES - POP QUIZ

1. If an English-speaking country is known as an anglophone country, what language would be spoken in a "hispanophone" country?

2. How many letters are there in the Hawaiian alphabet?
   a. 13
   b. 20
   c. 29
   d. 41

3. Switzerland has four official languages: French, German, Italian, and a local language called Romansch. But in what fifth language is the country's name written on its postage stamps?

4. Despite being the official language of just seven countries worldwide, Portuguese is the world's fifth-most spoken language, with more than 230 million speakers - most of whom live where?

5. What country has the most native English speakers?

6. What is the most widely spoken language in the Americas?

7. Luritja, Warumungu, and Warlpiri are native languages spoken in what country?

8. What tiny European country is the only country in the world to recognize Latin as one of its official languages?

WORLD LANGUAGES - POP QUIZ - SOLUTIONS

1. Spanish. The world's largest hispanophone country is Mexico.

2. A. 13. Incredibly, Hawaiian uses just A, E, H, I, K, L, M, N, O, P, U, W, and an apostrophe-like symbol called an 'okina (').

3. Latin. Swiss stamps bear the name Helvetia, to avoid prioritizing one of the country's actual spoken languages more than the others.

4. Brazil. With more than 200 million Portuguese speakers, 85% of the world's Portuguese - speaking people live in Brazil alone.

5. The United States. A quarter of a billion Americans speak English as their first language, with a further 60 million speaking it bilingually, or as their second language. In total, over 95% of the American population speaks English.

6. Spanish. There are roughly 400 million Spanish speakers in the Americas alone - that's four-fifths of the entire Spanish-speaking population of the world!

7. Australia. In fact, these are just three of the estimated 250–300 native Indigenous languages spoken there!

8. The Vatican City. There are even Latin-operated ATMs in the Vatican!

ANIMALS AND PLANTS

6. ANIMALS

○ The blue whale is not only the largest animal in the world, but it is also thought to be the largest animal to have ever lived on the planet!

- In fact, a blue whale's heart is the size of a car, and its tongue can weigh the same as a bull elephant.

- Most kangaroos are primarily left-handed.

- A hippo's skin is so thick the animals are essentially bulletproof.

- Giraffes have the same number of bones in their necks (seven) as humans do.

- Each zebra's pattern of stripes is as unique to them as our fingerprints are to us.

- Sharks do not have bones. Their internal skeletons are made entirely of cartilage.

- Cheetahs are well known to be the fastest land animals in the world, with a top speed of around 75 mph...

- ... but did you know that they can reach their top running speed from a standing start in just three seconds?!

- A lion's roar can be heard from five miles away.

- The world's biggest species of frog - the goliath frog of South America - can grow up to a foot in length and weigh as much as a domestic cat!

- Archeological evidence suggests humans have kept dogs as pets for more than 30,000 years.

- There are 40,000 muscles in an elephant's trunk.

- There is only one species of monkey in Europe, and they all live in Gibraltar!

- An average adult wolf can eat as much as 20 pounds of food in a single sitting...

- ... while an adult tiger can eat four times that much!

- Lions are not only found in Africa. A tiny, endangered population of so-called Asiatic lions live in the forests of Eastern India.

- Despite it being another name for the brown bear, the name "grizzly" actually comes from an old English word meaning "gray-haired"!

- A group of rhinoceros is known as a "crash."

- A typical kangaroo can move at more than 30 mph, and leap 25 feet in a single bound.

- Sperm whales can produce single clicks lasting just a fraction of a second - yet are so loud, they can be heard by other whales ten miles away.

- Some wolf packs have been known to preside over territories as big as 1,000 square miles!

- The longest-lived vertebrate creature is the Greenland shark. Some individuals have been estimated to be more than 500 years old!

- Tigers have white spots on the backs of their ears that mother tigers use to communicate with their cubs. They act as a flasher to the cubs to signal movement.

- Hippos have the largest mouth of any terrestrial animal and can open their jaw to almost 180°.

- Hippos also have enormously long tusk-like teeth - with the longest hippopotamus tooth ever recorded being an incredible 48 inches long!

- Because it holds its tail behind it, arched upward over its back, the squirrel is said to take its name from a Greek word that literally means "shadow-tail."

ANIMALS - POP QUIZ

1. What is a group of lions called?

2. All the wild penguins in the world live in which hemisphere - the northern or the southern?

3. Despite their names, killer whales are not whales. What kind of marine mammals are they?

4. Which of these creatures regularly sleeps more than 20 hours every day?

   a. Hyena
   b. Koala
   c. Giraffe
   d. Tiger

5. Echidnas and duck-billed platypuses are the only mammals in the world to do what?

6. What gigantic South American constrictor is the world's largest species of snake?

7. If geese is the plural of goose, what is the plural of mongoose?

8. What is the world's largest species of deer?

ANIMALS - POP QUIZ - SOLUTIONS

1. Pride. As the kings of the jungle, a group of lions has been known as a "pride" since the 15th century.

2. Southern. This means that despite both being polar creatures, polar bears and penguins never meet in the wild.

3. Dolphins. In fact, killer whales or orcas are the largest members of the dolphin family.

4. B. Koala. The koala's diet of eucalyptus leaves is so nutritionally poor they have very little energy resources and so live very sedentary lifestyles!

5. Lay eggs. An egg-laying mammal is known as a monotreme. Today, they are unique to Australia and New Guinea.

6. Anaconda. The largest wild anaconda ever recorded was reportedly around 33 feet in length and weighed over 800 pounds!

7. Mongooses! That is because the "goose" in mongoose isn't the bird, but an English spelling of an Indian word, mangus.

8. Moose. The moose is also the second largest land mammal in North America, after the bison!

7. BIRDS

- There are more than 18,000 different species of birds in the world.

- The ostrich is the world's largest bird. Individuals typically stand around seven to nine feet tall and can weigh more than 300 pounds!

- Ostriches also lay the biggest egg of any bird...

- ... but the Kiwi bird of New Zealand lays the largest egg relative to its body size. A single egg can weigh as much as one-fifth of the entire weight of an adult bird!

- Kiwi eggs are also among the most nutritious, as 60% of their contents are yolk.

- There are more than three times as many chickens in the world as there are human beings.

- The world's smallest bird is the Caribbean Bee Hummingbird. Also known as the zunzuncito, it is barely two inches long from tail to beak, and adults weigh less than a tenth of an ounce!

- Birds are the only living creatures to grow feathers.

- The peregrine falcon is thought to be the world's most widely distributed bird. They can be found on every continent except Antarctica.

- An ostrich's eye is bigger than its brain and is five times the size of a human eye.

- The Kori Bustard is the world's heaviest flying bird. Individuals can weigh more than 40 pounds but still get off the ground!

- The Wandering Albatross has the biggest wingspan of any living bird. From wingtip to wingtip, the birds typically measure a massive 12 feet across!

- Albatrosses use their colossal wings to travel far out to sea. In fact, individual birds can often go years without ever returning to dry land.

- An albatross named Wisdom was recorded breeding on Midway Island in the Pacific Ocean in 2021 and was found to be 70 years old, making her one of the oldest breeding vertebrates in the world!

- The world's largest predatory bird is the Andean Condor. Individuals can have a wingspan of around 11 feet and weigh more than 30 pounds!

- The marsh warbler - a tiny songbird native to Eurasia and Africa - is capable of mimicking the songs of around 80 other bird species.

- The enormous swirling flocks formed by starlings at dusk are known as murmuration's.

- Thanks to a statute enacted in the 12th century, all wild unclaimed mute swans in the United Kingdom are legally the property of the British royal family.

- Barn owls, ospreys, and bald eagles are among the many species of wild birds that mate for life and remain faithful to their partners for the rest of their lives.

- The world's smallest owl species is the Elf Owl, which grows to less than six inches in height and weighs less than one-and-a-half ounces!

- Woodpeckers strike their beaks against trees and timbers around 20 times every second!

- Tropical Hoatzin birds are born with a tiny claw in the middle of their wings to help them clamber around the branches.

- While some birds, like flamingos, sleep standing on one leg, other bird species have been found to sleep with one eye open, and others still sleep by shutting off one half of their brain at a time.

- Some bird species, including swifts and many far-travelling seabirds, like albatrosses, even manage to sleep while they are flying!

- A group of geese is called a gaggle when the birds are on the ground, but a skein when they are in flight…

- … while the V-shaped formation geese and similar birds make when they migrate is called a wedge.

- A pelican's pouch is properly known as a gular sac.

BIRDS - POP QUIZ

1. True or False? Despite being America's national bird, the bald eagle nearly went extinct in the 20th century.

2. What species of seabird completes the world's longest avian migration, traveling between the north and south poles every year?

3. The saggy featherless skin that hangs below a turkey's beak is called the "wattle." But what is the name of the drooping skin that hangs over the beak?

4. After the ostrich, what is the world's second-largest bird?

5. Why don't some species of vultures have feathers on their necks and faces?

   a. Because of how they fly
   b. Because of how they mate
   c. Because of how they eat
   d. Because of how they call

6. Some of the world's smartest birds include jays, magpies, and choughs. To what family of birds do they all belong?

7. The world's largest and tallest penguin species is also the world's deepest-diving bird. What is its name?

8. How many times does a hummingbird's heartbeat per minute?

   a. 60
   b. 120
   c. 480
   d. 1,200

BIRDS - POP QUIZ - SOLUTIONS

1. True! At one point in the 1960s, there were just 400 breeding pairs in the entire continental United States.

2. Arctic Tern. Despite having a wingspan of a little over a foot and weighing just four ounces, these tiny birds complete a 25,000-mile migration every year.

3. Snood. The wrinkling skin on the back of the turkey's head, meanwhile, is known as its "caruncles."

4. Emu. Standing around five feet tall, the emu is roughly two feet smaller than an ostrich - and of similar height to another flightless bird, the cassowary.

5. C. Because of how they eat. Having featherless skin stops the birds' plumage from getting smeared in blood when they feast on animal carcasses!

6. Crow (Corvids). Studies have shown crows can solve puzzles, manipulate tools, remember sequences, and even make rule-guided decisions!

7. Emperor penguin. Incredibly, emperor penguins are capable of diving to depths of more than 1,000 feet in the chilly waters of the Antarctic!

8. D. 1,200! Hummingbirds have one of the fastest heart rates in the animal kingdom.

8. IN THE WATER

○ All life on Earth started in the ocean…

○ … but evolutionary scientists now believe that some sea creatures were once land animals that returned to the sea. Whales, for instance, are distant relatives of deer, and walruses are related to otters!

○ There are more than 500 species of shark worldwide…

○ … all but seven of which are listed as endangered or vulnerable species.

○ The evolutionary record shows snapping turtles have barely changed in 90 million years, meaning they likely looked and hunted as they do today when dinosaurs were still around!

○ The Narwhal is a peculiar species of whale found in the Arctic with a long spiraling horn protruding from its head, which can reach up to ten feet long. It is thought that Narwhals were one of the creatures that may have inspired myths of legendary unicorns.

○ Despite its name, however, a Narwhal's horn is actually a gigantic tooth that grows from its mouth out through its skin!

○ Bowhead whales are some of the longest-lived sea creatures and can often live around 200 years.

○ …In fact, in 2007, a gigantic 50-ton Bowhead whale was caught off the coast of Alaska, with a century-old harpoon embedded in its neck!

○ Crocodiles and alligators have the strongest bites in the animal kingdom. While a typical human's bite force measures around 150 PSI (pounds per square inch), alligator bites measure more than 2,000…

- … while some species of crocodile have bite forces in excess of 5,000 PSI!

- One of the largest crocodiles ever recorded was a saltwater crocodile known as "Lolong" that grew to more than 20 feet long and weighed 2,370 pounds!

- Electric eels, which live in the freshwaters of the Amazon basin, can produce an electric shock of up to 860 volts and have been known to stun creatures as large as a horse!

- The Mantis Shrimp strikes its prey with its two large club-like claws at a speed of around 50 mph and a force equivalent to a gunshot from a .22 caliber rifle!

- All Clownfish are born male, with the largest fish in each brood typically changing sex to become the dominant female when required.

- Because sea otters sleep while floating on the surface of the sea, to prevent them from becoming separated while asleep, they interlock their hands to form large floating communities known as rafts.

- Bull sharks are among the most varied and versatile of sea creatures, and unlike many other shark species can easily switch between salt and fresh water. As a result, in tropical regions bull sharks can often swim up rivers, reaching far inland away from the sea!

- Starfish eat by turning their stomachs inside out and enveloping their food with them.

- They might have stomachs, but starfish lack brains, blood, and even anything resembling a central nervous system!

- Walrus tusks can grow to more than three feet in length.

O The sailfish is the fastest animal in the ocean. It can swim at speeds of around 70 mph - making it almost as fast as a cheetah!

O The Australian Box Jellyfish is the most venomous animal in the ocean. Their stings can cause paralysis and heart failure and are often lethal!

O Alligators cannot survive in salt water.

O If a shark stops swimming, it will drown.

O Some species of seals spend so much time in the water that they spend three-quarters of their lives holding their breath.

O All that holding their breath messes up a seal's body chemistry, however: some larger seals, including elephant seals, can have as much as 10% carbon monoxide in their blood, which would be toxic in humans.

O The Baikal Seal lives solely in Lake Baikal in central Asia. It is the only freshwater seal species in the world.

IN THE WATER - POP QUIZ

1. What is the name of the fin on the back of a fish or similar sea creature?

2. True or False? Lungfish are so-called because they do not have lungs.

3. What is unusual about the world's largest shark?
   a. It only eats plankton
   b. It lives in freshwater
   c. It has a beak
   d. It has red skin

4. The leatherback is the world's largest species of what kind of sea creature?

5. How many hearts does a squid have?

6. What kind of sea creature is known for being the only animal in the world in which the male gives birth?

7. True or False? All starfish have five limbs.

8. By what three-letter name is a school of dolphins also known?

IN THE WATER - POP QUIZ - SOLUTIONS

1. Dorsal fin. It is the dorsal fin that sharks often hold above the surface of the water as they swim!

2. False. In fact, they are so-called because they have an advanced lung system that allows them to breathe air almost like land animals do. When required - as in times of drought - lungfish can leave the water, protecting themselves by secreting a layer of mucus all over their body, and survive on land for up to a year!

3. A. It only eats plankton. The whale shark, ultimately, poses no threat to humans.

4. Turtle. Incredibly, an adult leatherback turtle can weigh as much as one ton!

5. Three. A squid has one so-called systemic heart, which pumps blood around its body like a human's, and two so-called branchial or gill hearts, positioned on either side of it, next to their gills.

6. Seahorse. After mating, the female seahorse deposits her eggs inside a special pouch in the male's body, and it is he who holds on to them until they hatch!

7. False. Some starfish have as many as 40 or 50!

8. Pod, which is also the name given to groups of other ocean creatures, including whales, seals, and sea lions.

9. PLANTS & TREES

- There are three trillion trees in the world…

- …but 15 billion trees are felled every year, and only five billion are planted.

- Trees grow from the top - which is why nest boxes and treehouses always remain at the same height!

- Counting the rings inside a tree to assess its age is a process known as dendrochronology.

- The world's oldest tree is a bristlecone pine in Nevada named Prometheus thought to be more than 4,900 years old.

- Unlike mammals and other creatures, trees never die of old age and all trees are capable of growing forever so long as they remain supplied with light and water, free from disease, and not harmed by floods, fires, or pests.

- The world's tallest known living tree is a Californian coastal redwood named Hyperion. It stands just over 380 feet tall!

- Because trees absorb carbon dioxide and produce oxygen, they can offset global carbon emissions. However, it would take a forest of 450 individual trees to offset the average carbon output of a single human being!

- In 1971, NASA took some tree seeds to the Moon on Apollo 14 and returned them to Earth to see if germinating in space would affect their growth. The trees they planted are now the property of the US Forestry Service.

- Some trees can form communities and are connected below ground, allowing them to share water and nutrition, and even alert one another to attacks by insects.

- Oak trees are struck by lightning more than any other tree species. No one knows why.

O Two-fifths of all the world's 64,000 species of trees grow in South America.

O There are 380,000 species of plants in the world - and 2,000 more are discovered every year!

O African baobab trees manage to survive dry seasons by storing water in their vast trucks. A single tree can store as much as 25,000 gallons of water!

O A single saguaro cactus of the American desert, meanwhile, can contain enough water to fill a bathtub 20 times!

O Venus fly traps work when a creature lands on them and touches a tiny hair lining inside of the trap's two hinged leaves. These highly sensitive hairs are properly known as trigger hairs.

O The spines on a cactus are not actually spines - they are modified leaves.

O The world's largest flower, the Rafflesia, can grow up to three-and-a-half feet in diameter. It grows in Borneo…

O … and because it attracts pollinating insects by secreting an odor similar to rotting meat, it is also known as the "corpse" flower!

O The world's smallest flowering plant is called Wolffia. It can reproduce by cloning itself, and if left unchecked could potentially continue reproducing until it cloaks the entire surface of the Earth!

O Despite its woody appearance, bamboo is actually a type of grass.

O A single blade of bamboo can grow as much as three feet in a single day!

○ Just under 97% of a cucumber is pure water.

○ Some flowers can move their flower heads from side to side throughout the day so that they follow the sun across the sky. This movement is known as heliotropism.

○ The world's tallest sunflower grew to a height of 30 feet.

○ The central trumpet-like tube of a daffodil flower is called the corona.

○ Of the world's flowering plants, 80% are pollinated by bees.

PLANTS & TREES - POP QUIZ

1. True or False? The majority of the world's plants are actually found in the ocean.

2. What is the national flower of England?

3. How thick can the bark grow on a giant sequoia?
   a. Three inches
   b. One foot
   c. Eighteen inches
   d. Three feet

4. What species of succulent plant is used to make tequila?

5. Digitalis is a toxin obtained from what popular flowering plant?

6. How much maple sap is required to produce one gallon of maple syrup?
   a. Five gallons
   b. Ten gallons
   c. Twenty gallons
   d. Forty gallons

7. Because of the large holes that grow naturally in its leaves, how is the plant Monstera Deliciosa better known?

8. Opium is obtained from what flowering plant?

PLANTS & TREES - POP QUIZ - SOLUTIONS

1. True! Around four-fifths of all the world's plant life are aquatic plants, including algae and seaweeds.

2. Rose. The rose has been England's national flower since the early Tudor period and the Wars of the Roses in the 1400s.

3. D. Three feet! Redwoods and sequoias have the thickest tree bark of all trees.

4. Agave. The plant is also used to make skin creams and hair treatments and can even be used to treat burns!

5. Foxglove. Despite their popularity in country gardens, foxgloves are actually poisonous - though foxglove poisoning is very rare.

6. D. 40 gallons! Some trees have even lower concentrations of sugar in their sap, and as much as 60 gallons will be needed to make a gallon of syrup!

7. Swiss cheese plant. It is also known as the "split-leaf plant" or "split-leaf philodendron."

8. Poppy. Or more specifically, the seed capsules of the poppy plant!

HISTORY

10. THE ANCIENT WORLD

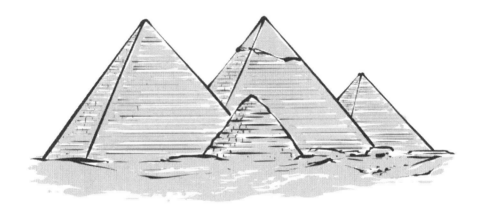

- The Ancient Egyptians worshipped more than 2,000 different gods and goddesses

- The pyramids of ancient Egypt were actually tombs, in which the pharaoh could be laid after his or her death, along with many of their belongings and everything they would need in the afterlife.

- The Great Pyramid at Giza was the world's tallest building until Lincoln Cathedral was completed in England in the 1300s.

- Each of the gigantic stone blocks used to build the pyramids weighed around two tons - that's as much as an elephant!

- There are more than 130 pyramids scattered around the Egyptian desert...

- ... but Egypt isn't the country with the most ancient pyramids. In fact, most of them are now found in neighboring Sudan.

- The word pharaoh literally means "great house" - thought to be a reference to the grand palace in which the kings and queens of Egypt lived.

- The Ancient Egyptians were fond of board games. One of their most popular was a game called senet, in which players took turns to move five pawns through 30 different squares, avoiding traps and forfeits along the way - rather like snakes and ladders!

- Because of unusual marks on his skeleton, some historians believe King Tutankhamun might have been killed by a hippopotamus or even a crocodile!

- The Ancient Egyptian empire reigned for so long - and the pyramids were built so long ago - that Queen Cleopatra, one of the last queens of Egypt, lived closer to our time now than to the construction of the Great Pyramid of Giza.

O The Great Pyramid of Giza is the only one of the Seven Wonders of the Ancient World that is still standing today.

O Despite being one of the greatest thinkers of the ancient world, the writings of Aristotle were almost lost after his death in 332 BCE - because they were stored in an old basement, and largely forgotten about!

O The Greek mathematician and philosopher Pythagoras was a strict vegetarian.

O The first Ancient Greek Olympics were held way back in 776 BCE...

O ... and the last before they were revived in the 19th century were held in 393 CE, under the European Emperor Theodosius the Great.

O The Ancient Greeks did not live entirely in what is now Greece but had overseas territories dotted across the Mediterranean, including what is now Italy, Turkey, and northern Africa.

O In parts of Ancient Greece, special votes could be held each year in which unpopular people could be ejected from the city and forced into exile...

O ... and the word the Greeks used for the shards of pottery on which the exiled people's names would be written - ostakon - is the origin of our word ostracism!

O The Ancient Greek polymath Archimedes invented the compound pulley, the screw pump (also known as an Archimedes screw) for raising water, and a fiendish military device called an Archimedes claw, which used a vast grappling hook to lift enemies' ships from the water.

○ The Ancient Greeks used to tell the time using the action of falling water: they invented a special kind of water clock called a "clepsydras."

○ The word "draconian," meaning especially severe, is derived from a stern lawmaker from Ancient Greece named Draco!

○ The Roman emperor Commodus was one of Rome's youngest serving emperors. He was only 16 when he took over from his father, Marcus Aurelius.

○ The Romans used to enjoy some bizarre dishes - including larks' tongues, stuffed dormice, and lamb brains!

○ The Roman emperor Nero is one of the most bizarre and controversial figures in the ancient world. In his short life (he committed suicide aged just 30) he supposedly ordered his mother to be killed and his wife to be killed and attempted to marry his favorite male slave!

○ The infamous Roman leader Caligula's name literally means "little boot"…

○ … while Cicero is thought to have taken his name from the Latin word for a chickpea.

○ After Rome was split in two in 395 CE, the Western Roman Empire only endured for another century or so - while the Eastern or Byzantine Empire survived until the mid-15th century!

THE ANCIENT WORLD - POP QUIZ

1. True or False? Julius Caesar was born by Caesarian section.

2. The Minoan civilization was entirely located on what Greek island?

3. What were there four of in Ancient Rome in 69 CE?

   a. Fires
   b. Emperors
   c. Earthquakes
   d. Wars

4. Who was the Greek equivalent of the Roman sea god Neptune?

5. The Roman Emperor Hadrian is known for building what gigantic structure across ancient England?

6. What destroyed the Roman city of Herculaneum?

7. Two of the months in our calendar are named after Roman emperors. Name either of them.

8. The Egyptian Ra was usually portrayed with the head of what animal?

THE ANCIENT WORLD - POP QUIZ - SOLUTIONS

1. False. There is a popular myth that Caesarian sections are named after him, but in Julius Caesar's time the only equivalent procedure always ended in the death of the mother - and Caesar's mother lived for many years after his birth.

2. Crete. The Minoans were one of the very earliest major civilizations in the history of Europe.

3. B. Emperors. Known as "The Year of the Four Emperors", 69 CE was a tumultuous one in Rome in which no less than four emperors ruled in quick succession: Galba, Otho, Vitellius, and Vespasian.

4. Poseidon. The Greeks and Romans had a great many equivalent gods and goddesses, and the two cultures were frequently confused. Zeus, Ares, and Aphrodite, for instance, were the equivalents of the Roman deities Jupiter, Mars, and Venus.

5. A wall. Hadrian's Wall was built in the 120s CE and stretches for an astonishing 73 miles (80 Roman miles) right across northern England.

6. A volcano. Herculaneum was the neighboring city to Pompeii, destroyed by Mount Vesuvius in 79 CE.

7. July (named for Julius Caesar) and August (for Emperor Augustus).

8. A falcon. Ra is one of the oldest recorded Egyptian gods. His depiction as a bird - and in particular, a falcon - relates to the fact that he was considered a god of the sun and the sky.

11. WORLD HISTORY

- The word Viking was not a regional term, but essentially a job title in ancient Scandinavia, equivalent to seafarer or privateer.

- China's Zhou dynasty is one of the longest-ruling dynasties in all world history. It remained in power in China for more than 700 years, from 1046 to 256 BCE!

- Shakespeare's famous play King Lear is said to have been based on the life of a genuine king known as Leir of Britain, who ruled over Ancient Celtic Britain in the 700s BCE.

- Constantine was the first Roman emperor to convert to Christianity, and as such was responsible for spreading the Christian faith across much of ancient Europe.

- Japan has the longest-established monarchy in the world. Although reliable historical records only date back to the 6th century, the Japanese royal family is said to have more than 2,600 years of lineage.

- Oxford University was founded before the Aztec Empire. (1096 – 1428)

- The famous Parthenon of Ancient Greece was commissioned back in the 5th century BCE by an Athenian statesman named Pericles the Great.

- The Code of Ur-Nammu is the oldest system of laws in known history. It was written in Mesopotamia more than 4,000 years ago!

- The Roman emperor Trajan was the first emperor in Rome's history not to have been born in Italy. In fact, he was born in Spain!

- The Ancient Egyptian ruler Thutmose III was such a talented soldier and military leader that he reportedly never lost a single battle during his 50 years in power.

- The Taj Mahal was originally intended to be a tomb.

- Damascus, in Syria, is said to be the world's oldest capital city. It was founded in 6000 BCE...

- ... though the area on which it is built may have been inhabited for as many as 10,000 years!

- It is impossible to visit the tomb of the first Qin emperor of China, Qin Shihuang, because his body is surrounded by pools of mercury!

- The famous Silk Route connecting tradespeople in Europe and Asia is properly known as the Network of Chang'an-Tianshan.

- The first European to make contact with Native Americans is said to have been a Spanish explorer named Juan Ponce de Leon. He encountered American natives in Florida in 1513.

- Despite its name, the Hundred Years War, fought between France and England, lasted 116 years.

- The world's oldest continually active university was founded in 1088 in Bologna, Italy.

- In the 1200s, the Mongol Empire expanded its reach across Asia so far that Mongol soldiers invaded several of the countries of eastern Europe - including Poland, Hungary, and Bulgaria!

- For a time in the Middle Ages, there were two popes. That's because schisms in the Catholic Church led to a rival pope being elected by those who opposed the papacy of Rome, and a second papal see established in the French city of Avignon.

○ The world's oldest cave paintings can be found in Chauvet Cave in the south of France. They date back to the Stone Age!

○ Some of the strangest named monarchs and rulers in history include the English king Ethelred the Unready, a 14th-century Austrian duke named Albert the Peculiar, the Polish crown prince Bolesław the Wry-Mouthed, and a Frankish king from the 8th century known only as Childeric the Idiot!

○ Mansa Musa, an ancient leader of the Malian Empire, is said to have been the richest person who has ever lived!

○ The gigantic stone statues found on Easter Island are known as moai. Some of them are more than 700 years old!

○ The longest-reigning ruler in history is said to be a Burmese king named Min Hti of Arakan. Although accounts of his reign are difficult to corroborate, it is possible he ruled for more than 95 years!

○ The Mongolian ruler Genghis Khan had so many children it has been estimated he has 16 million descendants living in the world today!

○ The Vikings are said to have been the first European people to have explored North America. A Viking sailor named Gunnbjörn Ulfsson arrived in Greenland in the 10th century CE!

WORLD HISTORY - POP QUIZ

1. Which ancient leader was known for his friendship (and possible romantic relationship!) with one of his generals, Hephaestion?

2. The famous Bayeux Tapestry is an embroidered depiction of what major historical event from 1066?

3. True or False? The Great Pyramid of Giza was the only one of the Seven Wonders of the Ancient World to be located in Africa.

4. Born sometime around the 6th century BCE, Thespis was the name of a famous what in Ancient Greece?

5. Which famous Russian ruler founded the Hermitage Museum in St. Petersburg in 1764?

6. On his voyage to the New World in 1492, Christopher Columbus set sail from Europe with three ships. But how many did he return with?

7. The Caral civilization is an ancient culture that emerged in South America more than 5,000 years ago. But in what country did it develop?

   a. Peru
   b. Chile
   c. Brazil
   d. Paraguay

Which famous English king died suddenly in 1199 when he was struck by a rogue arrow fired over a wall?

WORLD HISTORY - POP QUIZ - SOLUTIONS

1. Alexander the Great. Alexander and Hephaestion were childhood friends and remained close their entire lives, leading to much speculation about their exact relationship. They died within a matter of months of one another in 324–323 BCE.

2. The Norman Conquest of England. Thought to have been made in England within a matter of months or years of the Battle of Hastings - perhaps as a gift for William the Conqueror - the enormous Bayeux Tapestry is a staggering 230 feet long and, depicts no less than 58 separate scenes from the battle!

3. False. There was also the Pharos of Alexandria on the north coast of Egypt.

4. Actor. It's because of him that actors today are known as thespians!

5. Catherine the Great. Open to the public since 1852, the Hermitage is now one of the world's most popular museums, with almost three million visitors every year!

6. Two. One of his ships, the Santa Maria, sank on reefs off the coast of Haiti just months after his arrival in the Caribbean.

7. A. Peru. Despite being relatively little known today, the Caral people were historic contemporaries of the Ancient Egyptians!

8. Richard I (Richard the Lionheart). It has long been speculated that the arrow was mistakenly shot at the king by a young boy, sometimes identified as Pierre Basile.

12. US PRESIDENTS

- To date, 21 US states have been the birthplace of US presidents.

- The state that has been the birthplace of the most presidents is Virginia, where eight have so far been born, closely followed by Ohio, which is the home state of seven presidents.

- To date, 13 US states have only birthed one president each: Arkansas, California, Connecticut, Georgia, Hawaii, Illinois, Iowa, Kentucky, Missouri, Nebraska, New Hampshire, New Jersey, and South Carolina.

- After he retired from politics, George Washington opened a whisky distillery.

- Washington and James Monroe both ran in elections in which they had no opponent. (Needless to say, they both won!)

- In 1806, the future president Andrew Jackson shot and killed a man in a duel who had accused him of cheating in a bet.

- James Madison is the shortest president in history. He stood five feet four inches tall…

- … while the tallest president, Abraham Lincoln, was a foot taller, at six feet four inches!

- The first US president actually born in the United States was Martin Van Buren…

- … which is somewhat ironic, as Van Buren's family were Dutch, and he only spoke English as a second language. He remains the only president in history not to have spoken English as his mother tongue!

- President John Tyler had 15 children.

- President Zachary Taylor once admitted that before being on the ballot himself, he had never voted in a US election.

○ Chester A Arthur was the first left-handed president.

○ William Henry Harrison died of pneumonia just 32 days after his inauguration as president in 1841.

○ Rutherford B Hayes was the first president to have a telephone in the White House.

○ President Ulysses S Grant and his wife had been invited to the same theater show at which Abraham Lincoln was assassinated in 1845 but were forced to turn down the invite as they had already made plans to travel to New Jersey to visit family.

○ Grover Cleveland is the only president in history to serve two non-consecutive terms - so he is technically President Number 22 and Number 24!

○ President Ulysses S Grant once tried to annex the Dominican Republic to the United States.

○ The S in Ulysses S Grant's name didn't really stand for anything, and was the result of an error made on his application form to West Point...

○ ... Grant's real name, in fact, was Hiram Ulysses Grant, so his middle initial was actually U!

○ Oddly, the S in Harry S Truman's name didn't stand for anything either. It was meant as a tribute to both of Truman's grandfathers, both of whom had middle names starting with S!

○ Before he became an actor (and long before he worked in politics) Ronald Regan worked as a lifeguard...

○ ... while President Grover Cleveland once worked as a hangman!

○ When he took office in 1901, Theodore Roosevelt was the youngest person ever elected president at the age of 42.

○ William McKinley was once portrayed on an American $500 bill, but the McKinley bill was discontinued in 1969.

○ In 1910, William Howard Taft became the first sitting president to throw the opening ceremonial pitch at a Major League Baseball game.

○ Woodrow Wilson had just two years of political experience as governor of New Jersey before he was elected president in 1912.

US PRESIDENTS - POP QUIZ

1. Herbert Hoover was the first US president born west of the Mississippi. In what state was he born?

2. Which US president had the middle name Gamaliel?

3. Who is the longest-serving president in history?

4. Dwight D Eisenhower was the first president to ride in what mode of transportation?

   a. Hovercraft
   b. Tank
   c. Airplane
   d. Helicopter

5. Which US president was sworn in while on board Air Force One?

6. Calvin Coolidge is the only US president to have been born on what date?

7. Only three presidents in history have not kept pets. Name one of them.

8. Which president was known as "Old Rough and Ready"?

US PRESIDENTS - POP QUIZ - SOLUTIONS

1. Iowa. The 31st US president, Hoover was born in West Branch, Iowa, in 1874.

2. Warren G Harding. Surely one of the most unusual presidential names in history, Gamaliel is the name of a character mentioned in the New Testament.

3. Franklin D Roosevelt. Because of the events of World War II, FDR remained in power for a total of 4,422 days, from 1933 to 1945.

4. D. Helicopter. Eisenhower's flight took place on July 12, 1957, as part of a training exercise designed to test how quickly the president could be evacuated from the White House if necessary.

5. Lyndon Johnson. President Johnson was sworn in as quickly as possible after the assassination of John F Kennedy.

6. July 4! Meanwhile, John Adams, Thomas Jefferson, and James Monroe all died on July 4.

7. James K Polk, Andrew Johnson, and Donald Trump. (Although President Johnson apparently took to looking after the wild mice that lived in the White House!)

8. Zachary Taylor. The nickname was supposedly acquired during Taylor's military service.

13. KINGS & QUEENS

- The current royal family's surname is officially Mountbatten-Windsor.

- According to a 14th-century statute, any dolphin fished and caught in British waters is officially the property of the crown.

- The royal family's property portfolio includes six royal residences, almost all of London's famous Regent Street, and half the British shoreline.

- The British monarch is the only person in the United Kingdom who is permitted to drive without a license, without passing a test, and without having plates on their vehicle…

- … but not to worry - because the late Queen Elizabeth II was a fully trained mechanic and learned how to fix engines during active service in World War II!

- When a member of the royal family is traveling by airplane, it is customary for the plane to be stocked with a parcel of blood matching the royal's own in case an emergency transfusion is required while the plane cannot land.

- From William the Conqueror to King Charles III, there have been 42 officially recognized kings and queens of England, Great Britain, and now the United Kingdom.

- According to historical records at the time, William the Conqueror's corpse exploded when the attendants at his funeral tried to push it into his coffin.

- William the Conqueror's successor, William II, died in dubious circumstances that have never fully been resolved: he was shot through the chest with an arrow while hunting in 1100.

- When Richard I died in France in 1199, his heart was removed from his body and buried in Rouen.

O The medieval King of England Henry III once kept a pet polar bear at the Tower of London.

O Edward I's nicknamed was "the Hammer of the Scots" because of his repeated and violent attempts to see off rebellions from north of the English border.

O King John's official wardrobe records state that the king owned what we would now call a nightgown!

O King John is known for signing the important legal document called the Magna Carta back in 1215. Despite its age, several of the document's clauses remain law in the United Kingdom to this day.

O King Edward II made it illegal for anyone to wear a suit of armor in the British Houses of Parliament.

O To celebrate the coronation of Richard II in 1377, the water in the fountains of London was replaced with wine.

O Henry VI became king when he was just nine months old…

O … but went on to reign for 40 years. Oddly, his reign was split in two as he was deposed for a decade and reinstated in 1470.

O Edward V was king for just 78 days.

O The skeleton of King Richard III was found underneath a car lot in the English city of Leicester in 2012.

O The first English king to have his portrait put on currency was Henry VII, the father of Henry VIII.

O Despite being one of the most infamous kings in history, Henry VIII was never meant to come to the throne. He only became heir after his elder brother Arthur died unexpectedly.

○ In 1520, Henry VIII challenged the king of France, Francis I, to a wrestling match. Henry lost.

○ Elizabeth I used to celebrate Christmas by having life-size effigies of her friends made of gingerbread to decorate her palaces.

○ Queen Victoria's nine surviving children all married into the other royal families of Europe. This means the members of the British monarchy are all now distant relatives of most other European kings and queens. For that reason, Victoria is often known as The Grandmother of Europe!

○ Queen Elizabeth was the longest-reigning British monarch of all time.

○ King Charles III has his shoelaces ironed for him.

KINGS & QUEENS - POP QUIZ

1. Henry VIII married his sixth and final wife just four years before his death. What was her name?

2. Before Queen Elizabeth's record-breaking reign, who was England's longest-ruling queen?

3. Only two names in history have been shared by eight English kings. Name one of them.

4. And four names have only ever been used by one English king or queen since 1066. Name one of those two!

5. Every English king from 1714 to 1830 had what name?

6. Who is the only king in British history to have abdicated?

7. How old was Charles III when his mother, Elizabeth I, died in 2022?
   a. 53
   b. 63
   c. 73
   d. 83

8. There have been six royal houses or dynasties in England since 1066. Which one ruled from 1154 to 1485?

KINGS & QUEENS - POP QUIZ - SOLUTIONS

1. Catherine Parr. She went on to outlive him by another two years!

2. Victoria. Queen Victoria ruled from 1838 to 1901, a total of 63 years, seven months, and two days. Elizabeth II ruled for an incredible 70 years, seven months, and one day.

3. Edward, Henry. There has not been an English king named Henry since Henry VIII in the 16th century, while Edward VIII ruled briefly before his abdication in 1936.

4. Stephen, John, Anne, Victoria. If the week-long reign of Lady Jane Grey is counted too, then Jane can be added to this list as well!

5. George. Incredibly, this century-long period of history saw Britain ruled by four consecutive Georges, I–IV!

6. Edward VIII. King Edward ascended to the throne on the death of his father, George V, on January 20, 1936, and he abdicated on December 11, 1936. With a reign of just 326 days, he remains one of the shortest-ruling monarchs in British history!

7. C. 73. King Charles is now the oldest person in history to have ascended to the British throne.

8. Plantagenet. The Plantagenet Dynasty's three centuries in power is the longest ruling period of any British royal house.

14. BATTLES & WARS

- The marathon running race is named after a battle fought between the Greeks and the Persians in 490 BCE…

- … with the length of the race, 26 miles, said to be distance a soldier by the name of Pheidippides ran from the battlefield back to Athens to bring news of the Greek victory!

- In the 1st century CE, a series of battles called the Red Eyebrows Rebellion was fought in ancient China!

- One of the reasons historians believe the English lost the Battle of Hastings to the Norman French in 1066 is because they had fought another decisive battle just days earlier in the north of England. This meant they were exhausted from both fighting and marching south to see off the threat from across the Channel!

- Halley's Comet passed over the battlefield of the Battle of Hastings.

- In 1242, two rival factions of the European Orthodox church fought a battle in central Estonia on top of an entirely frozen lake!

- In the 14th century, the rival Spanish kingdoms of Castile and Aragon fought a conflict that became known as the War of the Two Peters, because both kingdoms were at the time ruled by kings named Peter…

- … while in the 1700s, Spain fought England in a conflict that became known as the War of Jenkins' Ear after an English Captain named Robert Jenkins claimed in England's House of Commons that his ear had been cut off by Spanish privateers in the Caribbean!

○ It is thought that the English king Henry V pawned some of the British crown jewels to pay for his invasion of France and the famous Battle of Agincourt in 1415.

○ The Wars of the Roses that took place in England from 1455 to 1485 were so called because the two rival sides - York and Lancaster - used a white and red rose respectively as their emblems.

○ The bloodiest battle ever fought on English soil was the Battle of Towton in 1461. Around half of the estimated 60,000 troops involved in the battle were killed …

○ … which means this one battle alone wiped out 1% of the entire population of England at the time.

○ In 1838, France and Mexico went to war over damage to a Mexican restaurant. It became known as the Pastry War!

○ The first shots fired in the American Revolutionary War were shot in Lexington, Massachusetts.

○ The very first clash of the American Civil War was at Fort Sumner in Charleston in 1861.

○ The Battle of Hampton Roads was not only the first naval battle of the Civil War but also the first battle between ironclad warships in human history.

○ Allan Pinkerton, the founder of the famous Pinkerton Detective Agency, worked in espionage during the Civil War and sent many of his agents undercover into spy on the Confederate Army.

○ Despite the war eventually taking over much of the continent, several major European countries remained officially neutral during World War I - including Switzerland, Spain, and Norway.

O Despite many people presuming German forces invaded Belgium first in World War I, two days before they crossed the Belgian border, they invaded the tiny landlocked nation of Luxembourg.

O The same day the United Kingdom declared war on Germany in 1914, the United States declared its neutrality.

O Because military vehicles were still relatively new, it has been estimated as many as five million horses were employed in World War I.

O At Christmas 1914, in the first year of World War I, an unofficial truce was observed along most of the Western Front in Europe, and British and German troops played a game of soccer in No Man's Land. (Germany won win 3–2!)

O On average during World War I, 6,000 men died every day...

O ... and it has been estimated that more than 4% of the entire French population at the time died in World War I.

O 25,000 miles of trenches were dug during the world wars.

O One of the most significant buildings destroyed by German air raids in World War II was Coventry Cathedral in Southern England. It had stood in the city of Coventry for more than 600 years.

O The average age of British troops involved in the Falklands War in 1982 was just 25.

BATTLES & WARS - POP QUIZ

1. What global conflict is said to have been triggered by the assassination of a previously relatively little-known European aristocrat and statesman named Archduke Franz Ferdinand?

2. True or False? The Eighty Years War did not last 80 years.

3. The Civil War Battle of Bull Run was fought on July 21, 1861. But what is "Bull Run"?

4. Despite many people presuming it to be a myth, the existence of which ancient city - the site of a ten-year war fought against an alliance of Greek city-states - is now supported by archaeological evidence?

5. Although its photographer has never been identified, there is a very famous picture of a protester holding bags of shopping and standing in front of a tank during a Chinese rebellion in 1989 - in what famous square?

6. Which African county became landlocked when its northern coast broke away to form the independent Republic of Eritrea in 1991?
   a. Gabon
   b. Ethiopia
   c. Tanzania
   d. Uganda

7. Before World War II broke out, how was World War I known?

8. How many target beaches were involved in the Normandy Landings of 1944?

BATTLES & WARS - POP QUIZ - SOLUTIONS

1. World War I. Despite being little known outside of his home country of Austro-Hungary, the fallout from the duke's death saw a chain of countries declare war on one another, eventually sparking the first worldwide conflict in history.

2. False. Unlike the Hundred Years War, Europe's Eighty Years War was fought for precisely the length of time its name refers to - eight decades, from 1568 to 1648.

3. It's a stream in Virginia. The First Battle of Bull Run was the first major battle of the entire Civil War.

4. Troy. The city of Troy is now identified as a ruined city in present-day Hisarlik, in northwest Turkey.

5. Tiananmen Square. Not only is the photographer unknown, but the identity of the protester in it is unknown too. As a result, he has become known simply as "Tank Man"!

6. B. Ethiopia. Eritrea is now one of the world's most recently formed nations — while Ethiopia is one of the last countries in history to have become landlocked due to the breakaway of a neighboring state!

7. The Great War. The earliest record of the Great War, being referred to as "World War I", dates from the same year in which the conflict ended — 1918.

8. Five. The beaches covered a 50-mile stretch of the Normandy coast and were given the codenames Utah, Omaha, Gold, Juno, and Sword.

SPORTS

15. HISTORY OF SPORT

O One of the earliest sporting pursuits was ice skating, evidence of which dates back more than 4,000 years....

O ... when early Europeans made ice skates using shinbone fragments instead of metal blades!

O The Romans used to play a game similar to soccer, using an inflated pig's bladder as a ball!

O Golf was invented in Scotland more than 500 years ago but might have its origins in a Dutch game played even earlier.

O The earliest written record of a sport named "football" comes from a law of 1457 that made it illegal!

O In jeu de paume - a Tudor period game from which modern tennis evolved - players didn't use rackets and typically slapped the ball with their open hands!

O The earliest record of a game of cricket being played dates from 1597.

O Games resembling baseball have been played since at least the 1700s...

O ... but the rules of the game as itis today were not codified until the New York Knickerbocker Baseball Club was founded in 1845!

O Lacrosse is America's oldest team sport. Its origins lie with the Native Americans, but the sport first proved popular among colonists in the 1850s.

O Rugby football is named after a British public school in Warwickshire where it was invented in the 1840s.

O One of the earliest literary records of baseball comes from Jane Austen's 1817 novel Northanger Abbey.

- Basketball was invented by a YMCA fitness instructor named James Naismith in 1891.

- Originally Naismith's rules didn't specify a maximum number of players per side, as he just wanted to get as many people involved as possible. But because 18 people used to regularly show up to play his games, that was the number that stuck!

- Britain's famous Grand National horse race was first run in 1839…

- The America's Cup yacht race was first competed in 1851…

- .. and the first Open Golf tournament was played way back in 1860!

- The first codified rules for soccer were outlined at Cambridge University in 1848.

- The first American football match was played on November 6, 1869.

- In 1844 two Native American participants at a swimming competition in London introduced the front crawl to a European audience.

- The first organized game of ice hockey was played in North America in 1875.

- One of the world's first official governing bodies was the FIG, or International Gymnastics Federation. It was founded in Liege, Belgium, in 1881!

- Judo was developed in Japan in 1882.

- William Morgan invented the sport of volleyball in Springfield, Massachusetts…

- … and originally called it "mignonette"!

○ Prizefighting boxing was only made legal in the United States in 1920 by the state of New York, with other states quickly following suit.

○ The Olympic Games were reintroduced in 1896 and competed in Athens for the first time in 1,500 years!

HISTORY OF SPORT - POP QUIZ

1. What Japanese martial art literally means "empty hand"?

2. Spencer Gore was the first winner of the men's singles title in what world-famous tennis competition back in 1877? And…

3. … True or False? In the late 1800s, Spencer Gore was also a famous horse racer.

4. American football was conceived of as a combination of what two existing ball games?

5. The first modern Olympic Games were held in Athens. Where were the second held in 1900?

6. What indoor sport was known as "whiff-whaff" in Victorian England?

   a. Squash
   b. Table tennis
   c. Handball
   d. Fencing

7. The official stones used to play what Winter Olympic sport are all made from granite obtained from a single quarry in Scotland?

8. How long after the invention of basketball was netball invented?

   a. One day
   b. One week
   c. One month
   d. One year

HISTORY OF SPORT - POP QUIZ - SOLUTIONS

1. Karate. The "kara" in karate is the same as in karaoke - which literally means "empty orchestra"!

2. Wimbledon.

3. False. As well as being the first Wimbledon champion, he was a renowned cricket player!

4. Soccer and rugby. The invention of American football is credited to Walter Camp, a Yale University athlete and coach.

5. Paris. The city also hosted in 1924, and a century later in 2024, becoming the second city in history to host the modern Olympic Games on three occasions.

6. B. Table tennis. Like "ping-pong," the name "whiff-whaff" was meant to replicate the sound of the ball being knocked back and forth!

7. Curling. Most of the curling stones used in the Olympics have been made from granite mined on Ailsa Craig, a tiny island in Scotland's Firth of Clyde.

8. D. One year. The idea was to make the sport more accessible for women.

16. AMERICAN FOOTBALL

- American football's 17-week season is one of the shortest of all professional team sports.

- The most career points scored by an NFL player are the 2,673 points made by Adam Vinatieri between 1996 and 2020...

- ...while Vinatieri also scored more than 100 points in a record 21 seasons!

- The biggest attendance at a game of American football in history was in 2016, when more than 130,000 people watched a game between the University of Tennessee Volunteers and Virginia Tech Hokies.

- In 1929, Chicago Cardinals player Ernie Nevers scored 40 points in a single game against the Chicago Bears. His score remains the most points scored for a single player in American football history.

- Helmets did not become mandatory in the NFL until 1979.

- Companies typically pay around $7 million to broadcast a television commercial during the Super Bowl.

- The first televised NFL game was on October 22, 1939.

- The longest field goal ever scored was 66 yards, made by the Baltimore Ravens' Justin Tucker in 2021.

- The Seattle Seahawks' name was chosen in a public competition in 1975.

- In 1916, college team Georgia Tech scored 222 points in a single game of football...

- ... including a record 32 touchdowns!

- In 2021, the longest football game in NCAA history - which ran to a record nine overtimes - took place between the Illinois Fighting Illini and Penn State Nittany Lions.

- The Green Bay Packers are unique in that their name was established in 1919 and has never been changed - nor has the team relocated - ever since.

- Tom Brady has well-earned his nickname as the GOAT, or Greatest of All Time. He has appeared in more Super Bowls - a total of ten - than any other player...

- ... he has won more Super Bowls - a total of seven - than any other player...

- ... and is the oldest player to have ever played in and won a Super Bowl!

- In Super Bowl LII in 2018, the teams covered the highest combined total number of yards - 1,151 - in NFL history.

- Between 1992 and 2010, quarterback Brett Favre made a record 297 consecutive starts.

- The Arizona Cardinals had the longest post-season victory drought in NFL history, covering 76 seasons from 1947 to 1998...

- ... while the New England Patriots scored the longest winning streak in the NFL, taking 21 games between 2003 and 2004.

- In 2021, when the Tampa Bay Buccaneers took on the Kansas City Chiefs at the Raymond James Stadium in Tampa, Florida, for Super Bowl LV, it was the first time in NFL history that a team had played a Super Bowl at their home stadium!

○ The most career touchdowns in NFL history is 208. Jerry Rice set the record in 303 games, and played for the San Francisco 49ers, Oakland Raiders, and Seattle Seahawks from 1985 to 2004.

○ The NFL's most successful coach is Don Shula, who oversaw 347 victories for the Baltimore Colts (1963–69) and the Miami Dolphins (1970-95) in a career spanning four decades.

○ NFL quarterback George Blanda played in a record 26 seasons of professional football in his 40-year career.

○ Jason Hanson played a record 327 games for the same team - the Detroit Lions - between 1992 and 2012...

○ ... while the record for the most consecutive games played for the same team was set by Jim Marshall of the Minnesota Vikings, who played 270 games in a row between 1961 and 1979.

AMERICAN FOOTBALL - POP QUIZ

1. Of the 20 most-watched television broadcasts in American history, how many of them are Super Bowls?

   a. One
   b. Five
   c. 13
   d. 19

2. Which NFL legend has thrown a record 89,214 regular season passing yards?

3. In 2013, who won a record fifth NFL MVP title?

4. Which is the only team in NFL history to have scored an undefeated season in the Super Bowl?

5. In what decade did Doug Williams of the Washington Redskins become the first African American quarterback in NFL history to start in the Super Bowl?

6. Which NFL team has won the most games all time?

7. Name two of the three NFL teams based in California.

8. How many US states are home to an NFL team?

   a. 13
   b. 23
   c. 33
   d. 43

AMERICAN FOOTBALL - POP QUIZ - SOLUTIONS

1. D. 19! The only other broadcast that comes close is the final episode of M*A*S*H*, broadcast to an audience of 105 million people in 1983.

2. Tom Brady. Including postseason games, Brady threw his record 100,000th passing yard in 2022!

3. Peyton Manning. He had previously won in 2003, 2004, 2008, and 2009.

4. Miami Dolphins. They did so in 1972.

5. 1980s. Williams was in the starting lineup of Super Bowl XXII, in 1988.

6. Green Bay Packers. The Packers also have the second-highest win–loss record (.571) in NFL history behind the Dallas Cowboys (.576).

7. Los Angeles Rams, Los Angeles Chargers, San Francisco 49ers.

8. B. 23. While 27 states have no NFL team, 16 have one, five have three (Ohio, Pennsylvania, New Jersey, Maryland, and Texas), and two have three (California and Florida).

17. BASEBALL

○ A regulation baseball must be nine to nine-and-a-quarter inches in circumference and weigh between of five and five-and-a-quarter ounces...

○ ... while a baseball bat must be no more than two and three-quarters inches in diameter at its thickest, no longer than 42 inches, and weigh no more than 36 ounces.

○ Historically, however, before these regulation weights and measures were introduced, some baseball bats weighed as much as three pounds.

○ The distance between the bases on a baseball diamond is 90 feet.

○ Baseball was originally played without gloves. One of the first players to adopt the practice was Doug Allison, a catcher for the Cincinnati Red Stockings...

○ ... but he only began wearing a glove in 1870 when he injured his hand and wanted to protect it from the ball!

○ The average baseball match lasts just under three hours...

○ ...but the actual gameplay, on average, lasts just 18 minutes!

○ The fastest MLB game in history lasted just 51 minutes. It was played between the New York Giants and Philadelphia Phillies back in 1919...

○ ... but the longest in history, between the Chicago White Sox and Milwaukee Brewers in 1984, took just over eight hours.

○ The song "Take Me Out to the Ball Game" was written in 1908.

○ Baseball mounds are typically made of a mixture of raw silt clay and sand.

○ The record number of home runs scored by a single player in a baseball game is four. To date, more than a dozen NLB players have reached this landmark - the first of whom was Bobby Lowe back in 1894!

O In the 2022 MLB season, 3,356 pitches above 100 mph are thrown - more than in any season in history!

O The fastest pitch of all time was thrown by the Cincinnati Reds' Aroldis Chapman. He threw the ball at 105.8 mph against the San Diego Padres in 2010.

O Joe DiMaggio's legendary hitting streak lasted for an astonishing 56 games!

O The first team to wear numbers on their jerseys was the New York Yankees back in the 1920s.

O The first World Series took place in 1903.

O Because early baseballs were often softer and more loosely stitched, the early years of professional baseball - typically up to the 1920s - is known as the "Dead Ball Era."

O Baseball was an Olympic sport from 1992 until 2008 before it was removed from the official roster of disciplines before the 2012 Games in London.

O Nolan Ryan pitched a record seven no-hit games over his 20-year career, from 1973 to 1991.

O One of the strangest trades in baseball history took place in 1931 - when the Chattanooga Lookouts traded shortstop Johnny "Binky" Jones to the Charlotte Hornets in exchange for a 25-pound turkey.

O When Babe Ruth was traded to the Yankees for $100,000 in 1919, it was an unheard-of amount at the time. In modern terms, the cost price is equivalent to $1.7 million.

○ Only one player in MLB history has died after being struck by an errant pitch during a game. The tragedy occurred in 1920, when Cleveland Indians' Ray Chapman was accidentally but fatally struck in the head by Yankees pitcher Carl Mays.

○ The MLB record for striking out in a nine-inning game is five times—and it has been achieved more than 150 times since records began in 1901!

○ Yogi Berra's real first name is Lawrence.

○ On August 4, 1982, Joel Youngblood made history when he became the first player in MLB player to get hits for two different teams in two different cities on the same day. He started the day playing for the New York Mets, was traded to the Montreal Expos after the game, and then debuted for them that evening in Philadelphia.

BASEBALL - POP QUIZ

1. In 1890, Harry Stovey became the first player in recorded baseball history to reach what career milestone?

2. Murders' Row was a nickname given to a seemingly unbeatable raft of players who played for what team in the late 1920s?

3. Which St. Louis Cardinals left fielder holds the record - 50, across the 1989–90 season - for most consecutive stolen bases without getting caught?

4. Joey Votto, Alex Rodriguez, Chipper Jones, Wade Boggs, and Darrell Evans all scored a home run on..., what?
   a. Their 40th birthdays
   b. Christmas Day
   c. July 4
   d. Thanksgiving

5. Which early 1900s Hall of Famer scored a record 792 doubles over 22 seasons?

6. What Baltimore Orioles manager was ejected from a record 91 games?

7. In 1939, who became the first MLB player to have his number retired?

8. True or False? Both Babe Ruth and Lou Gehrig were struck out in succession during an exhibition game by a 17-year-old girl.

BASEBALL - POP QUIZ - SOLUTIONS

1. 100 career home runs. Stovey set his record - a major milestone at the time - for the Boston Reds on September 3, 1890, in a game against Cleveland.

2. New York Yankees. The nickname was especially used of the first six hitters of the Yankees 1927 lineup: Earle Combs, Mark Koenig, Babe Ruth, Lou Gehrig, Bob Meusel, and Tony Lazzeri.

3. Vince Coleman. National League Rookie of the Year for 1985, Coleman is also the only MLB player in history to steal over 100 bases in three consecutive seasons: 1985 (110), 1986 (107), and 1987 (109).

4. A. Their 40th birthdays. MLB legends Darrell Evans (1988) and Jim Thome (2011) also scored homers on their 41st birthdays!

5. Tris Speaker. Speaker also had one of the best career batting averages in MLB history, .3447.

6. Earl Weaver - who led the Orioles for 17 years - was even once thrown out of both games of a double header!

7. Lou Gehrig. Gehrig's Number 4 was retired on the same day he made his famous "luckiest man alive" speech on July 4, 1939.

8. True! Jackie Mitchell was a 17-year-old female pitcher for the Chattanooga Lookouts.

18. BALL SPORTS

- A game of basketball was originally only half an hour long. The game's inventor, James Naismith, first proposed two 15-minute halves, with a five-minute break in between.

- The longest recorded game of volleyball was played in the Netherlands in 2011. It lasted 85 hours!

- The longest game of tennis ever played at the Wimbledon Championships lasted 11 hours and was played over three days in 2010, between John Isner and Nicolas Mahut. The final set alone lasted eight hours and 11 minutes, with Isner eventually winning 6–4, 3–6, 6–7, 7–6, 70–68!

- In a standard game of table tennis, the ball is struck more than 120 times per minute and can travel across the net at as much as 70 mph.

- Tennis balls were originally white. The color was changed to a neon yellowish green in the 1980s to make the ball easier to track on television.

- A score of zero is thought to be known as "love" in tennis because the 0 figure has the same shape as an egg - or l'oeuf in French!

- The longest table tennis rally in history lasted 11 hours and 50 minutes. It was played by two Australian players in Dubai in 2020.

- According to history, rugby was invented during a soccer match in 1823 when a player named William Webb Ellis picked up the ball and ran with it!

- Around 55,000 tennis balls are used every year during the Wimbledon Championship.

- The rules of basketball originally forbade dribbling: as in netball, a player receiving the ball had to remain in place until they threw it to one of their teammates...

- ... until dribbling was officially introduced to the rules of the sport in 1891!

- The first basketball was actually a soccer ball!

- When tennis first proved popular in the Victorian era, women would play in full floor-length skirts, with sleeves, high collars, and stockings underneath.

- A single volleyball player will jump 300 times in a single game...

- ... while in a typical match, a tennis player will run a total of three miles across the court!

- The fastest rugby try in a professional game was scored by Vula Maimuri of Fiji against the New Zealand Crusaders at a match in Christchurch in 2001 just 12 seconds into the game!

- Beach volleyball is nothing new - it was first played in Hawaii in 1915!

- 98% of professional squash players are college graduates.

- The indentations on a golf ball are called "dimples." There is no set rule for the maximum or minimum number of dimples on a competition golf ball, although most usually have around 350–400...

- ... although the maximum ever imprinted on a ball was 1,070!

- The grass on the tennis courts of Wimbledon is kept at precisely 8 mm (one-third of an inch) tall. It is an especially hardy type of rye grass.

- The world's biggest soccer stadium is in North Korea. The Rungrado 1st of May Stadium has a capacity for 114,000 people and is the home stadium of the secretive nation's national team.

- The world's biggest stadium overall, however, is the Narendra Modi Stadium in Ahmedabad, India, which is home to the Indian national cricket team. It can house 132,000 spectators!

- The fastest recorded tennis serve was played by Australian Sam Groth at a competition in Busan in 2012. The ball was served at 163.4 mph!

- It has been estimated that the world's most popular sport is soccer, with more than three billion fans and players.

- The world's second-most popular sport is debatable, with hockey, volleyball, and golf all vying for the title - but in terms of the number of spectators and fans, cricket is popularly said to come in second place!

- The fastest swing speed of any bat sport is field hockey. Male players can strike the ball mid-game at more than 100 mph.

BALL SPORTS - POP QUIZ

1. It has been estimated that the average golfer has around a one in 12,500 chance of… what?

    a. Being struck by lightning
    b. Scoring a hole in one
    c. Being hit by another player's ball
    d. Landing in a bunker

2. What team ball sport has positions called gully, silly mid-on, silly mid-off, forward short leg, and the nightwatchman?

3. Since table tennis was added to the official roster of events at the 1988 Olympic Games, what country has won every single title?

4. Which tennis player won his record 24th Grand Slam title in 2023?

5. Which legendary golfer, who has won more than 80 PGA tournaments, scored his first hole in one aged eight?

6. What wood are all professional cricket bats made from?

7. Before the current ball was adopted in the 20th century, historically what ball sport was once played with solid beechwood balls, feather-stuffed leather balls known as "featheries," and solid balls called "gullies"?

8. Professional tennis can be played on four different surfaces. Name two of the four categories that the International Tennis Federation recognizes.

BALL SPORTS - POP QUIZ - SOLUTIONS

1. B. Scoring a hole-in-one. It's been estimated that the chances of a golfer being struck by lightning is roughly one in 250,000 - so if you're a golfer, luckily, you're 20 times more likely to score a hole in one!

2. Cricket. There are lots of fielding positions in cricket known as "silly," about how close the players must stand to the player batting - and so how foolishly liable they are to be hit by the ball!

3. China. Incredibly, China has picked up more than ten times the number of gold medals as their closest competition in Olympic table tennis, South Korea.

4. Novak Djokovic. Djokovic also holds the record for the greatest number of weeks as the World Number 1 tennis player, amassing his 400th week at the top in 2023.

5. Tiger Woods. Incredibly, Woods was the top-ranked golfer in the world for 264 consecutive weeks from August 1999 to September 2004, and then again for a record 281 consecutive weeks from and again from June 2005 to October 2010.

6. Willow. Specifically, cricket bats are made from white willow wood treated with raw linseed oil to give them greater strength.

7. Golf. "Gully" golf balls were made of dried and solidified sapodilla sap.

8. Clay, grass, carpet (artificial), hard. Despite their name, clay courts are mainly composed of crushed stone and brick, which gives them their orange color.

19. THE OLYMPICS

- The Olympic Games originated in Ancient Greece in the 8th century BCE.

- The original Olympics were held every four years for more than 1,000 years until they were banned by Emperor Theodosius I in the 4th century CE, along with all other events and festivals that were considered to be pagan in early Christian Europe. It would be another 1500 years before the Games were revived.

- The idea of bringing the Olympic Games back into the modern world was that of Pierre de Coubertin, a French aristocrat and historian who was also an early President of the modern International Olympic Committee.

- When the Olympic Games were revived in the late 1800s, some of the first events included tug of war and rope climbing.

- Only 14 countries took part in the first modern Olympic Games in 1896.

- Originally, winners at the modern Olympics were given silver medals, and those in second place were given copper medals...

- ... because the gold, silver, and bronze arrangement was not put in place until 1904.

- Back in Ancient Greece, however, medals were not used at all: winners were given a laurel wreath instead.

- Although the 2020 Games were delayed due to the COVID-19 pandemic, the Olympics have only officially been canceled three times in history, and in each instance because of war: in 1916, 1940, and 1944.

- The 1940 Games were especially dramatic as they had originally been awarded to Tokyo. After the outbreak of the war, the

Games were shifted to Helsinki in Finland, and then canceled altogether!

○ All the canceled host cities later went on to host the games at a later date. Berlin (the planned host city in 1916) hosted the 1936 Games instead; Tokyo hosted the first of its two Olympics in 1964 (having lost the 1940 Games); and Helsinki hosted for the first time in 1952.

○ At just under 450 miles from the Arctic Circle, Helsinki remains the northernmost city to have hosted the Summer Olympics.

○ The first city in the world to host the modern Olympic Games three times was London, in 1908, 1948, and 2012.

○ Although it is customary for the ruling head of state to open the Olympic Games, at the 1904 Games in St Louis, President Roosevelt was unavailable, so the Games were opened by the city's mayor.

○ Although the 1908 Games were held in London, the sailing events that year were held 300 miles away off the coast of southern Scotland!

○ In 1976, Princess Anne, one of the late queen's children and a sister of Charles III, became the first member of the British royal family to compete in the Olympic Games.

○ The first brothers to win Olympic gold medals were Americans John and Sumner Paine, who came first in two shooting events at the 1896 games in Athens.

○ Only four countries in history have taken part in every modern Olympics since 1896: Greece, Australia, France, and Great Britain.

○ Among the dozens of cities that have bid for but never been awarded the Olympic Games are Chicago, Istanbul, Madrid, and Philadelphia.

○ Los Angeles has made a record ten Olympic host bids, more than any other city, and has been successful three times: it hosted in 1932, 1984, and will host for a third time in 2028.

○ Other cities that have made multiple bids include Rome (which hosted in 1960 and has bid nine times), Paris (which has hosted three times, in 1900, 1924, and 2024, and bid six times), and Amsterdam (which hosted in 1928 and has made six bids).

○ The most unsuccessful city in terms of Olympic bids is Detroit. It has bid seven times - in 1944, 1952, 1956, 1960, 1964, 1968, and 1972 - but has never been awarded the Games.

○ When the 2016 Games were hosted by Rio de Janeiro, it was the first time in history that the Olympics had been held in South America.

○ If Winter Olympic Games are included, the country that has hosted the most Olympics in the modern era is the United States. Including the forthcoming 2028 Games in Los Angeles, it has hosted nine Summer and Winter Olympics in 1904, 1932, 1984, 1996, 1932, 1960, 1980, 2002, and 2028.

○ Golf, rugby, baseball, and softball were all originally discontinued as Olympic disciplines, but have recently been added back into the official roster of events in the 21st century.

○ Among the sports that have been contested at the Olympics in the past but are no longer competed are polo, cross-country running, lacrosse, motor boating, and croquet!

○ One of the most peculiar Olympic disciplines in history was the standing high jump - in which competitors would leap over a high jump bar from a standing start, rather than taking a run up! It was included as an Olympic sport at every Games from 1900 to 1912, before being discontinued.

THE OLYMPICS - POP QUIZ

1. The Winter Olympics were not introduced at the same time as the modern Summer Olympic Games. In what decade did they start?

2. Since 1928, it has been a tradition for what country to enter the Olympic stadium first during the opening ceremony's Parade of Nations?

3. And which country is it now traditional to enter last in the opening ceremony?

4. Although today it is the 100 m, what is the shortest sprinting distance that has ever been competed at the Olympic Games?

   a. 20 m
   b. 40 m
   c. 60 m
   d. 80 m

5. What US swimmer holds the record for the most Olympic medals by an individual in history?

6. Who is the only person in history to have officially opened the Olympic Games twice, in 1976 and 2012?

7. German Olympian Franziska van Almsick holds the record for the most career medals without ever winning gold. In what discipline did she compete, from 1992 to 2004?

8. What was the first Summer Olympic Games in history to be held in the host nation's winter season?

THE OLYMPICS - POP QUIZ - SOLUTIONS

1. 1920s. The first Winter Games were held in Chamonix, France, in 1924.

2. Greece.

3. The host nation. The remaining countries enter the stadium in alphabetical order, in the official language of the host nation.

4. C. 60 m. The 60 m dash was an official Olympic sport just twice, back in 1900 and 1904. The Olympic record is 7.0 seconds, set by American athlete Alvin Kraenzlein in Paris in 1900.

5. Michael Phelps. Phelps holds the record for both the highest number of gold medals (23) and total medals (28) for any individual in Olympic history.

6. Queen Elizabeth II. As well as the 2012 Games in London, as the head of state of Canada the late queen also opened the 1976 Games in Montreal. Incredibly, the queen's father George VI (London, 1948), her late husband Prince Philip, the Duke of Edinburgh (Melbourne, 1956), and her great-grandfather, Edward VII (again London, 1908) all opened the Olympic Games too!

7. Swimming. Incredibly, Van Almsick won a total of ten Olympic medals - four silver and six bronze - without ever achieving gold.

8. Rio de Janeiro, 2016. The Rio Games were also the first held in South America, and the first held in a Portuguese-speaking country.

20. GAMES & PASTIMES

- The oldest known chess set dates from 900 CE. It was made in India.

- The proper name for the hobby of collecting stamps is philately, while a stamp collector is a philatelist.

- Other words for collectors and enthusiasts include an arctophile (a collector of teddy bears), deltiologist (a collector of postcards), phillumenist (a collector of matchboxes), tegestologist (a collector of beermats), and scripophile (a collector of stock and share certificates).

- Chess is a compulsory school subject in Armenia.

- In the Polish version of Scrabble, Z is worth one point.

- There are around 1,000 possible openings to a game of chess.

- The character on the front of a Monopoly box is called Milburn Pennybags.

- The character you operate on in a game of Operation is called Cavity Sam.

- The murder victim in a game of Clue is called Mr. Boddy (but was called Dr. Black in the United Kingdom version, Cluedo!).

- The word TWELVE is worth 12 points in a game of Scrabble.

- Originally, snooker only had five colored balls (red, yellow, green, pink, and black). The blue and brown balls were only added later.

- The line a darts player must stand behind to throw is called the oche.

- The most productive set of letters in a game of Scrabble is AEINRST. It can be rearranged to play nine different seven-letter words: anestri, antsier, nastier, ratines, retains, retinas, retsina, stainer, and stearin.

○ There is around a 15% chance that the seven tiles you pick out of the bag at the start of a game of Scrabble will be able to spell a seven-letter world.

○ Chess has been played for at least 1,500 years...

○ ... but the alternating black and white board was only introduced in the late 11th century.

○ Potentially, the highest-scoring word that could be played in a game of Scrabble is the chemical name oxyphenbutazone...

○ ... but that would mean playing your seven tiles across eight tiles already located on the board, in such a way that you hit all three possible triple-word scoring squares in a row! In the unlikely event that that would indeed happen, oxyphenbutazone would score you 1,778 points!

○ Games resembling checkers have been played for over 5,000 years.

○ The Russian chess player Garry Kasparov became the youngest World Chess Champion in 1985 when he was just 22 years old...

○ ... but the world's youngest chess grandmaster was crowned in 2021: American player Abhimanyu Mishra was just 12 years old at the time!

○ In a game of Scrabble, K is the only tile worth five points.

○ At the very beginning of a game of chess, there are eight possible ways to put your opponent in mate within just two moves.

○ The highest possible break in a game of snooker is 147 points...

○ … and at the 1997 World Championships, British snooker star Ronnie O'Sullivan scored 147 in just five minutes and 20 seconds.

○ There are more possible games of chess than there are atoms in the known universe.

○ In 2015, the official French-language Scrabble championship was won by New Zealander Nigel Richards. He didn't speak French and had only started to learn the French word list two months before the competition.

GAMES & PASTIMES - POP QUIZ

1. Who was depicted on the world's first postage stamp when it was introduced in 1840?

2. At the start of a game of chess, how many squares have playing pieces on them?

3. What popular board game was originally known as "tables" in medieval Europe?

   a. Chess
   b. Ludo
   c. Backgammon
   d. Checkers

4. Priced at $400, what is the most expensive property on a traditional New York Monopoly board?

5. Chaturanga is an ancient Indian game now recognized as the possible origin of what popular board game?

6. What kind of puzzle does a cruciverbalist enjoy?

7. True or False? Scrabble was invented by an English schoolteacher.

8. What curious number is the total of all the figures on a roulette wheel?

   a. 123
   b. 666
   c. 999
   d. 1313

GAMES & PASTIMES - POP QUIZ - SOLUTIONS

1. Queen Victoria. Known as the Penny Black, Britain's first postage stamp established the tradition of using a profile portrait of the reigning monarch, which has continued ever since.

2. Exactly half -32. There are 64 squares on an 8x8 chess board, and as each player starts with eight pieces and eight pawns, there are two sets of 16 pieces on each side!

3. C. Backgammon. The "gammon" in backgammon comes from gamen, a Middle English word for a game.

4. Boardwalk. The cheapest property, meanwhile, is Mediterranean Avenue at $60.

5. Chess. Incredible, Chaturanga is thought to have been played in India for more than 5,000 years!

6. Crossword. Although crossword puzzles date back to the early 1900s, the word cruciverbalist was only coined as recently as 1971.

7. False. Actually, it was invented by an American architect named Alfred Mosher Butts.

8. 666. There are 36 digits on a roulette wheel, not including the zero!

ART AND ENTERTAINMENT

21. LITERATURE

- Agatha Christie is popularly said to be the bestselling literary author of all time. Her 85 novels have sold an estimated three billion copies worldwide!

- The single bestselling book of all time is the Bible.

- JRR Tolkien and CS Lewis - the authors of the Lord of the Rings and The Lion, the Witch, and the Wardrobe - were best friends.

- The earliest known use of the word "hobbit" in print dates from 1897 - 40 years before JRR Tolkien's book was published!

- And 65 years before Dr Seuss wrote How The Grinch Stole Christmas, Rudyard Kipling used the word "grinch" as a verb meaning to crush or grate in 1892.

- The English novelist Enid Blyton, known for the Famous Five books, published 762 books in her lifetime!

- Roald Dahl was inspired to write Charlie and the Chocolate Factory because British chocolate company Cadbury used to send boxes of chocolates to his school as a child to test.

- In none of Arthur Conan Doyle's novels, Sherlock Holmes ever says, "Elementary, my dear Watson."

- Dr. Seuss wrote Green Eggs And Ham after his publisher bet him that he couldn't write a story using no more than 50 different words.

- JD Salinger had an early draft of The Catcher in the Rye in his bag with him when he took part in the Normandy Landings in 1944.

- John Steinbeck's original manuscript for Of Mice and Men was eaten by a dog…

- ... while Stephen King's debut novel Carrie was fished out of his bin by his wife after he originally discarded it!

- Despite popular belief, there are not 1,001 stories in the Arabian Nights collection. The 900 or so stories instead were said to have originally been read over 1,001 nights.

- In an early version of Edgar Allen Poe's "The Raven," the bird that repeatedly croaks "nevermore" was going to be a parrot! But...

- ... it's possible that a chance meeting with Charles Dickens convinced Poe to change his mind, as Dickens had a pet raven at the time.

- Bibliosmia is the name given to the scent of old books.

- Harry Potter creator, JK Rowling, is popularly said to be the first author in history to make $1 billion from book sales alone.

- Ray Bradbury's original title for his classic novel Fahrenheit 451 was The Fireman...

- ... while Jane Austen's original title for Pride and Prejudice was First Impressions.

- Wizard of Oz author L Frank Baum came up with the name "Oz" because one of the file cabinets in his office was labeled O–Z.

- Lewis Carroll's Alice in Wonderland was originally banned in China because it includes talking animals.

- Victor Hugo's novel Les Misérables contains an 800-word sentence.

- Charles Dickens is said to be the most cinematically adapted novelist of all time...

- ... but the most performed literary character on the silver screen is popularly said to be either Count Dracula or Sherlock Holmes.
- A novel written in the form of a series of letters is called an epistolatory novel.
- Frankenstein's Monster isn't called "Frankenstein." The only name by which it is referred to in the original novel is "Adam."
- All the profits from JM Barrie's novel Peter Pan were donated to a children's hospital in London.

LITERATURE - POP QUIZ

1. What are the two cities in Dickens' novel A Tale of Two Cities?

2. Which of these famous literary lines is never actually used in its original story?

   a. "Please sir, I want some more."
   b. "Me, Tarzan. You, Jane."
   c. "Et tu, Brute?"
   d. "Call me Ishmael."

3. True or False? George Eliot was a woman.

4. Which three famous authoress sisters had a brother called Bramwell?

5. The most expensive book ever sold was purchased by Microsoft founder Bill Gates in 1994. Which famous Renaissance scientist wrote it?

6. What happened to two-and-a-half million copies of unsold romance novels in the UK in 2003?

   a. They were anonymously mailed to Buckingham Palace
   b. They were buried under a road
   c. They were burned on the beaches of Dover
   d. They were pulped to make Harry Potter novels

7. True or False? Ian Fleming took the name James Bond from a famous ornithologist.

8. What eponymous Roald Dahl character takes her name from a poem by Hilaire Belloc?

LITERATURE - POP QUIZ - SOLUTIONS

1. London and Paris. A Tale of Two Cities is popularly said to be the best-selling novel in literary history, with an estimated 200 million copies sold since its publication in 1859.

2. B. "Me, Tarzan. You, Jane." Tarzan never says this line in any of Edgar Rice Burroughs' original books.

3. True. Her real name was Mary Ann Evans.

4. The Brontë Sisters. Bramwell shared his sisters' creativity but was a painter and poet rather than an artist. All four siblings died remarkably young: Bramwell died of tuberculosis in September 1848 - just a few months before his sister Emily died of the same disease, followed by Anne in the spring of 1849, and Charlotte in 1855.

5. Leonardo da Vinci. The Codex Leicester is a collection of da Vinci's scientific papers and writings.

6. B. They were buried under a road. The books were used as foundations for the reconstruction of an M6 motorway.

7. True! Fleming needed a name for his character and saw a book on his shelf entitled Birds of the West Indies by James Bond.

8. Matilda. Dahl was partly inspired to write the book after reading Belloc's poem "Matilda Who Told Such Dreadful Lies."

22. THEATER

- Modern theater was developed in Ancient Greece. Back then, audiences tended not to clap to show their appreciation, but stamp their feet!

- "Encore!" literally means "again" or "once more" in French, so implies that a performance has been so good you would like to see it again!

- "Bravo!" meanwhile means "brave" in Italian. Originally used only for operatic performances, it is sometimes changed to "brava" (feminine) when the performer is female and "bravi" (plural) for an ensemble performance.

- Shakespeare wrote 37 plays.

- At the time of Shakespeare's life, acting was an exclusively male profession. So even some of his most famous female roles, including Cleopatra and Romeo and Juliet, would have originally been played by men!

- Shakespeare is known to have collaborated on some of his work with other contemporary playwrights. He in return also worked on their plays, and scholars today can recognize his style of poetry and prose in other writers' works.

- Shakespeare was also an actor and performed with a theater troupe known as the "King's Men."

- The famous Elizabethan playwright Christopher Marlowe, who wrote Doctor Faustus, was killed in a brawl at a London tavern in 1593. He was just 29 years old.

- The earliest record of the character Father Christmas comes from a play written by one of Shakespeare's contemporaries, Ben Jonson.

- Ben Jonson was convicted of killing an actor named Gabriel Spenser in 1598.

- Jonson escaped the death penalty (which was still in action in England at the time) through a legal loophole called "Benefit of the Clergy," in which he only had to read a Bible verse to show his literacy. Instead of being hanged, Jonson was branded on his thumb and released.

- After his death some 39 years later, Ben Jonson was buried standing up at Westminster Abbey, possibly because they were short on space!

- When Shakespeare's Globe Theatre burned down in 1613, nobody was injured except for a man whose trousers caught fire...

- ... and the man put them out with a bottle of beer!

- The word "background" was originally a theatrical term, used for the rearmost part of a stage, the greatest distance from the audience.

- While the protagonist of a play is the most important character, the second-most important is called the "deuteragonist."

- The fire at the Globe itself was believed to have been started by a misfiring stage cannon.

- JM Barrie's classic story Peter Pan was originally written as a play for children in 1904. The fairy character of Tinkerbell was produced on stage by someone in the wings holding a mirror next to a lamp and reflecting a circle of light against the backdrop.

- The foremost part of a theatrical stage is called the "apron." By definition, the apron is the part of the stage that extends beyond the "proscenium" - the archway that divides the auditorium from the stage area.

O The word "explode" originally meant to clap or jeer a performer off the stage. It is an etymological cousin of the word "applaud"!

O The author Thomas Hardy was a keen theater fan - but the only acting role he ever played in his life was a walk-on part in a Christmas pantomime.

O Arthur Miller's father lost everything in the stock market crash of 1929.

O Before he became a famous playwright, Tennessee Williams worked as a waiter, a factory worker, and a caretaker on a chicken ranch. He later called his work on the chicken farm "disastrous."

O One of Williams' earliest breaks as a writer was winning $100 in a playwrighting contest for under 25-year-olds...

O ... except he had lied about his age and was actually 27 at the time!

O Eugene O'Neill originally hated his masterpiece play A Long Day's Journey into Night, and after completing it in 1941 admitted to a friend that he never wanted to see it published or performed.

O Samuel Beckett was an accomplished cricketer.

THEATER - POP QUIZ

1. Shakespeare was inspired to write which of his plays after hearing of a ship that had been wrecked in a tropical storm off the island of Bermuda?

2. Samuel Beckett's play Waiting for Godot ends with two characters exchanging the lines, "Well, shall we go, then?" / "Yes, let's go." The play's final stage direction says… what?

3. Shakespeare's plays are traditionally divided into three categories. Name two of them.

4. What masterpiece of 20th-century American theater was originally due to be called Blanche's Chair in the Moon?

5. Which famous English crime and murder mystery writer wrote the world's longest-running play, The Mousetrap?

6. What was unusual about Shakespeare's father?

   a. He could not read or write
   b. He was also called William
   c. He was the Lord Mayor of London
   d. He was an actor

7. True or False? Shakespeare's Globe Theatre did not have a roof.

8. An 18th-century actress named Charlotte Charke is said to be the first woman ever to play what legendary male theatrical role?

   a. Hamlet
   b. Macbeth
   c. Romeo
   d. Othello

THEATER - POP QUIZ - SOLUTIONS

1. The Tempest. The Sea Venture was wrecked in 1609 while sailing to Virginia.

2. "They do not go." Like many of Samuel Beckett's later and most popular works, Waiting for Godot was originally written in French as En attendant Godot.

3. Comedy, Tragedy, History. Some of Shakespeare's plays - like Twelfth Night and Much Ado About Nothing - straddle the boundaries between comedy and tragedy, and so have also been labeled "problem plays."

4. A Streetcar Named Desire. The Blanche in question is the play's tragic heroine, Blanche DuBois.

5. Agatha Christie. Incredibly, The Mousetrap celebrated its 25,000th performance on November 18, 2012, and is still going strong!

6. A. He could not read or write. Despite his son being the most famous writer of all time, John Shakespeare was illiterate.

7. True! At least part of its roof is thatched, but the main auditorium is largely open-air.

8. B. Hamlet. Charke's performance was followed just weeks later by a highly acclaimed performance by the legendary West End actress Sarah Siddons.

23. ART & ARTISTS

O Salvador Dali designed the Chupa Chups logo.

O Leonardo da Vinci was able to write with one hand while drawing with the other simultaneously.

O In the famous 1930 portrait American Gothic by Grant Wood, the couple is meant to be father and daughter, not husband and wife...

O ... but their relationship and the picture itself are fictional. Wood actually modeled the couple on his sister, Nan, and the family dentist, Byron McKeeby!

O Pablo Picasso had a pet owl. He found the bird injured one day and nursed it back to health.

O Vincent van Gogh's famous Starry Night painting depicts the view from the insane asylum in Provence where he was institutionalized for a time in the 1890s.

O There are actually five versions of Edvard Munch's famous painting, The Scream, including a pastel version, a lithographic print, and two crayon and tempura versions.

O The German title under which Munch's The Scream was originally displayed was The Scream of Nature.

O The earliest picture of someone wearing spectacles was painted by an Italian artist named Tommaso da Modena in 1352.

O The Mona Lisa is painted onto a panel of poplar wood, not a canvas.

O Although it is now arguably the most famous painting in the world, the Mona Lisa was not widely known until it was stolen from The Louvre in 1911.

O Van Gogh only sold one painting during his lifetime.

- The lady in the Mona Lisa painting has been identified as an Italian noblewoman named Lisa del Giocondo.

- After the death of his brother, Dali became convinced that he was his brother's reincarnation.

- When Henri Matisse's painting Le Bateau was first exhibited in New York, it was hung upside down...

- ... and the mistake was not spotted for six weeks!

- Van Gogh fell in love with his cousin, Kee. In response, his uncle banned him from their family home!

- When asked why he had never painted a self-portrait, the artist Gustav Klimt answered, "There is nothing special about me."

- Andy Warhol's 32 Campbell's Soup prints are displayed in New York's Museum of Modern Art in chronological order - but not in the order Warhol painted them, but beginning with the soup Campbell's introduced to the American market first...

- ... That's because, despite them being some of his most famous paintings, Warhol never left specific instructions about how he wanted them displayed!

- Pietà, a 1499 sculpture by Michelangelo, is the only one of his works that the artist himself signed. He later saw his name on his work as a sign of ego and pride, he and never signed another work again.

- The rich blue pigment ultramarine was once so expensive that many artists could only use it very sparingly. The exception was when painting the robes of the Virgin Mary, which are often shown to be ultramarine in color as a sign of sacrifice and devotion by the artist.

○ Comedian was a 2019 artwork by an Italian artist named Maurizio Cattelan. It consisted of a banana duct taped to a wall…

○ … but in 2020 - while Comedian was on display at an art fair in Miami - performance artist David Datuna ate it. The banana was replaced later the same day.

○ The most expensive painting in the world is da Vinci's Salvator Mundi. It was sold at auction in 2017 for $450 million (equivalent to more than half a billion dollars today).

○ The French artist Paul Cézanne was known for his wild fits of temper at what he saw as his own failings when his paintings did not work out, and he would often rip up or throw away his works before they were complete…

○ … in one instance, he was found trying to retrieve a canvas from the branches of a large tree after he had thrown it up there in frustration.

ART & ARTISTS - POP QUIZ

1. True or False? Leonardo da Vinci's surname is Vinci.

2. How long did it take Michelangelo to paint the ceiling of The Sistine Chapel?
   a. Four days
   b. Four weeks
   c. Four months
   d. Four years

3. Which French artist's painting, Impression, Sunrise, is the reason why he and artists sharing his style are now known as "Impressionists"?

4. Whose 1888 painting Café Terrace at Night, painted in the town of Arles in France, has proved so popular that the town has replicated the painting in real life so that tourists can stand in the same spot as the artist and see an identical café and terrace today?

5. Leonardo da Vinci's famous Last Supper painting is often wrongly described as a fresco, but it is technically a... what?

6. Which famous Florentine family is believed to have commissioned Botticelli to paint The Birth of Venus?

7. True or False? Michelangelo's David is life-size and stands just over six feet tall.

8. Which French artist - known for his paintings made from thousands of individual dots, rather than brushstrokes - is said to have used more than 200,000 dots in his famous painting A Sunday Afternoon on the Island of La Grande Jatte?

ART & ARTISTS - POP QUIZ - SOLUTIONS

1. False. Leonardo was actually born in the Florentine town of Vinci in Italy, hence the name by which he has become known simply means "Leonardo of Vinci."

2. D. Four years. He worked from 1508 to 1512.

3. Claude Monet. Monet chose the title for his work because he thought its haziness gave it only the "impression" of a sunrise, rather than a more realistic depiction.

4. Vincent Van Gogh. The spot in which he sat to paint Café Terrace at Night was one of Van Gogh's favorite haunts in Arles. After completing the painting, he wrote to his sister that, "I enormously enjoy painting on the spot at night."

5. Mural. Frescos are painted onto wet plaster walls, while murals are produced on a dry service.

6. Medici. Botticelli painted The Birth of Venus in the 1480s, perhaps having been commissioned by Florentine banker and politician Lorenzo di Pierfrancesco de' Medici.

7. False. Although it can be difficult to tell how large it is from photographs, as anyone who has seen the statue themselves will explain, it is actually 17 feet tall!

8. George Seurat. The technique of painting using dots that blur together from a distance is known as pointillism.

24. MUSIC

○ Musical notes have two names - one is a system based on fractions and numbers, popular in North America, and the other is based on Latin prefixes, popular in Europe. The way that the Latin prefixes are arranged means that the note known as a 64th note in America is ultimately known as a hemidemisemiquaver in Europe!

○ JS Bach once wrote a cantata (an arrangement for voices and orchestra) inspired by his love of good coffee.

○ Mozart kept a pet starling.

○ Doctors trying to cure Beethoven's deafness once suggested he take daily baths in the river at the bottom of his garden.

○ Giacomo Puccini, the composer of operas like Madame Butterfly and La Bohème, loved driving speedboats…

○ … and his interest in modern technology led to him becoming Thomas Edison's pen pal!

○ Scott Joplin performed at the 1893 Chicago World's Fair. His success there helped to make ragtime piano one of the most popular styles of music in turn-of-the-century America.

○ Buddy Holly's breakout hit "Peggy Sue" was originally called Cindy Lou.

○ Elvis Presley had an identical twin brother, but he died shortly after birth.

○ Michael Jackson's album Thriller is believed to have sold 70 million copies worldwide and is credited with being the best-selling album of all time.

○ The first Black woman ever to be the cover star of Rolling Stone was Tina Turner.

- Freddie Mercury was born in Zanzibar, an island in Tanzania off the east coast of Africa.

- Bob Dylan is thought to be the only person in history to have won an Oscar, a Grammy, and a Nobel Prize. He has also been awarded the Presidential Medal of Freedom.

- For one week in 1964, the Beatles held all five slots on the Billboard 100.

- On the cover of the Beatles' album Help! the Fab Four are each making a different semaphore letter. Despite many people presuming they are spelling H-E-L-P, the letters they are actually producing read N-U-J-V!

- The Beach Boys were originally called "The Pendletones."

- Liquid paper was invented by Bette Nesmith Graham, the mother of Michael Nesmith of The Monkees.

- The first song David Bowie ever recorded was called "I Never Dreamed," in 1963. It was long presumed to have been lost, until he discovered it stored in a breadbox when he was moving house in the 1990s.

- Bill Wyman was originally only invited to join the Rolling Stones because he owned an amplifier, and the band didn't have one.

- Madonna has an IQ of 140.

- Beyoncé's lucky number is four, because it is her birthday, her husband's birthday, and her mother's birthday.

- Mariah Carey's vocal range covers five octaves. It ranges from the note F2 (two Fs below middle C on a piano) to an astonishing G7 (four Gs above middle C) -higher than many famous opera singers, including Maria Callas.

151

O Despite being Canadian, Celine Dion once represented Switzerland in the Eurovision Song Contest.

O Sheryl Crow wrote her James Bond theme "Tomorrow Never Dies" in 15 minutes.

O Coldplay was originally called Starfish.

O Lady Gaga learned to play the piano by ear when she was four years old.

O Taylor Swift's middle name is Alison.

MUSIC - POP QUIZ

1. Which legendary artist - —known for producing three of the most successful albums of all time, Michael Jackson's Off the Wall, Thriller, and Bad - has won 28 Grammy Awards?

2. True or False? Elvis never performed live outside of North America.

3. Pop artist Andy Warhol designed the front cover of what classic album by the Rolling Stones?

4. The BBC banned the Beatles' song "I Am The Walrus" because its lyrics included what word, which the corporation deemed indecent?

   a. Knickers
   b. Brassiere
   c. Underpants
   d. Y-fronts

5. Who made history when they won their record 32nd Grammy Award in 2023?

6. In 2012, what song became the first music video to reach one billion views on YouTube?

7. Which rock group, fronted by Michael Stipe, were originally known as Twisted Kites?

8. All orchestras tune to the note A, which is traditionally produced by what woodwind instrument as a reference point for other musicians to tune to at the start of a performance?

MUSIC - POP QUIZ - SOLUTIONS

1. Quincy Jones. Incredibly, Jones has been nominated for 80 Grammy Awards in his career!

2. True! Elvis performed a handful of shows in Canada and traveled to Europe for military service, but he never performed outside of North America.

3. Sticky Fingers. The artwork famously features a closeup of the waist and crotch of a pair of jeans - but despite what many fans presume, the model was not Rolling Stones' frontman Mick Jagger!

4. A. Knickers. The song was banned immediately after its release in 1967!

5. Beyoncé. She overtook legendary conductor Sir Georg Solti to become the most decorated artist in Grammy history.

6. "Gangnam Style." Two years later, it also became the first song in history to amass two billion views!

7. R.E.M. One of the most popular and acclaimed rock bands of their time, R.E.M. was founded as Twisted Kites in Athens, Georgia, in 1980. Stipe reportedly picked the band's replacement name, R.E.M., at random.

8. Oboe. The oboe produces the orchestra's tuning note because its tone is so sharp and clear, so it can easily be heard by the other players.

25. CINEMA

O The first movie ever to win the Best Picture Academy Award was the World War I saga Wings in 1928.

O The Oscars were originally a private function, conducted over little more than an hour, with the winners informed of their success before the awards were handed out!

O Although Judy Garland's slippers are ruby red in the movie, in the book of The Wizard of Oz, they are silver. The moviemakers wanted to take full advantage of their color technology, and so changed them for the film!

O Both Bette Davis and Katharine Hepburn were considered for the role of Scarlett O'Hara in Gone with the Wind before it eventually went to Vivien Leigh.

O The famous playwright George Bernard Shaw won an Oscar for the adapted screenplay of his play Pygmalion, which was made into a film in 1938...

O ... but he wasn't pleased. In fact, Shaw wanted nothing to do with Hollywood, nor the movie adaptation, and called the award an "insult" to his original work!

O On the poster for the classic movie Casablanca, Humphrey Bogart is shown wearing a fedora and a trench coat - the picture doesn't come from Casablanca but was painted based on a still from another of his movies, Across the Pacific!

O The first person to win an Oscar for a Shakespearean adaptation was Sir Laurence Olivier. He won Best Actor and, as producer, Best Picture, for his role in Hamlet in 1948.

O The Oscars were first broadcast on television in 1953.

O The climactic chariot race scene in the 1959 adaptation of Ben-Hur required 15,000 extras.

- The opening scene of The Sound of Music - in which Maria is seen singing in a grassy field high in the Alps - had to be reshot several times because the downdraft from the helicopter used to film it kept blowing Julie Andrews off her feet!

- The "blood" seen being washed down the bathtub plughole in Alfred Hitchcock's Psycho was actually chocolate sauce.

- Psycho was also the first movie in Hollywood history to show a toilet being flushed.

- The cast of Francis Ford Coppola's Godfather movies was almost very different: the studio wanted Laurence Olivier to play Vito Corleone (not Marlon Brando) and suggested Robert Redford instead of Al Pacino to play his son Michael.

- When his movie career failed to take off as he had hoped, Harrison Ford retrained as a carpenter and was working as such when he was cast in Star Wars.

- The Vietnam War epic Apocalypse Now was originally planned to take six weeks to shoot. In the end, it took a year and a half.

- The puppet shark used in the movie Jaws was nicknamed "Bruce" by the crew.

- Inside the model of E.T. in the Steven Spielberg movie was a two feet ten inches stuntman.

- Anthony Hopkins won the Best Actor Oscar in 1992 for his role as Hannibal Lecter in The Silence of the Lambs - despite his character appearing on screen for just 16 minutes…

- …, but his is still not the shortest Oscar-worthy performance in movie history! In 1977, Beatrice Straight won the Academy Award for Best Supporting Actress, despite appearing on screen in the movie Network for just five minutes!

- The sound of the T-rex's growl in Jurassic Park is partly made by slowing down the growl of a koala bear.

- The singing voice of Jack Skellington in Tim Burton's The Nightmare Before Christmas is that of Danny Elfman - the film's composer.

- Before Kate Winslet was offered the role, Gwyneth Paltrow, Winona Ryder, Claire Danes, and Reese Witherspoon were all considered to play Rose in Titanic...

- ... while Jared Leto, Matthew McConaughey, Chris O'Donnell, and Stephen Dorff were all considered for the role of Jack that eventually went to Leonardo di Caprio.

- The movie Toy Story 2 was almost deleted from Pixar's servers before it was completed when a glitch began automatically undoing the computer-generated movie's code.

- When Parasite was named Best Picture at the 2020 Oscars, it became the first non-English-language film to win the award in history.

- In the summer of 2023, it was announced that the Marvel Cinematic Universe had so far grossed $30 billion.

CINEMA - POP QUIZ

1. In the Lord of the Rings movies, which actor, who played Aragorn, accidentally broke his foot when he kicked a helmet on screen - with the moment being kept in the final film?

2. Both Heath Ledger and Joaquim Phoenix won Oscars for playing what comic book character?

3. What was the name of the gigantic diamond that features in the 1997 movie Titanic?

4. What was the name of the blue monster voiced by John Goodman in Monsters, Inc. whose two million hairs were programmed to respond naturally as he moved?

5. Only three movies in Oscar history have won the so-called "Big Five" of Best Picture, Best Director, Best Actor, Best Actress, and Best Screenplay. Name one of them.

6. Which actress, who won an Oscar for Silver Linings Playbook, was almost cast in Kristen Stewart's role as Bella in the Twilight movies?

7. True or False? Gone with the Wind producer David O Selznick was fined for the use of foul language in Clark Gable's line, "Frankly, my dear, I don't give a damn."

8. For what movie did Katharine Hepburn win her record-setting fourth acting Oscar in 1982?

CINEMA - POP QUIZ- SOLUTIONS

1. Viggo Mortensen. The scene was kept in the second movie in Peter Jackson's acclaimed trilogy, The Two Towers.

2. The Joker. At the age of just 28, Heath Ledger died the year before the ceremony at which he won the Best Supporting Actor Academy Award in 2009. His family attended the ceremony in his place and accepted his award on stage.

3. The Heart of the Ocean. As realistic as it looks on screen, the diamond itself was just a prop and was actually made of cubic zirconia.

4. Sully. At the time of the movie's production, Sully was the most complex CGI-animated character in movie history!

5. It Happened One Night (1934), One Flew Over the Cuckoo's Nest (1975), and The Silence of the Lambs (1991).

6. Jennifer Lawrence. Actress Lily Collins was also screen-tested for the role - while Chronicles of Narnia star Ben Barnes was considered for the role of Edward Cullen that eventually went to Robert Pattinson.

7. False. The idea that Selznick was fined $5,000 for this swear has persisted as a Hollywood legend for almost a century! But the truth is that the rules governing bad language in the movies were changed shortly before the film's release, allowing lighter curse words in certain contexts.

8. On Golden Pond. Hepburn had earlier won awards for Morning Glory (1934), Guess Who's Coming To Dinner (1968), and The Lion in Winter (1969).

SCIENCE

26. THE HUMAN BODY

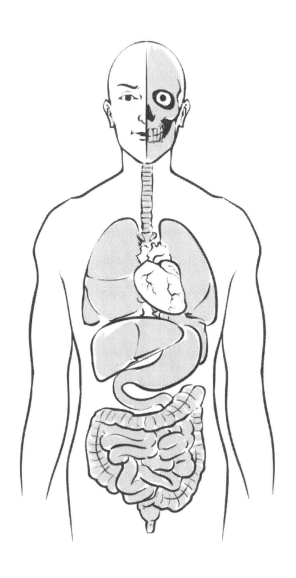

- Your body replaces 50,000 cells every three seconds.
- There are 206 bones in an adult skeleton...
- ... 64 of which are in the arms and hands, and 60 of which are in the legs and feet.
- Babies have fewer bones than adult humans.
- The longest bone in the human body is the thighbone (femur).
- You are taller in the morning than in the evening.
- Just like your fingerprints, your tongue has a unique "print" of taste buds that is different from everyone else's.
- By the age of 60, the average person has lost half of the taste buds on their tongue.
- Women's hearts beat faster than men's hearts.
- It takes 17 different muscles to form a smile...
- ... but twice that many to frown. So smiling is easier!
- Our eyes never grow - which is why babies' eyes seem so much larger, as their bodies have not grown around them to match!
- The colored part of the eye, the iris, is actually a ring of muscle that controls the size of the pupil.
- The tongue is the only muscle in the human body not attached at both ends.
- People blink less when they're lying - but after they've finished talking, will tend to blink more.
- The cornea of the eye is also the only part of the body without an internal blood supply. It actually gets all the oxygen it needs to function from the air.

- When you blush, the reaction in your body not only turns your cheeks red but makes the lining of your stomach flush too.

- There are more bacteria in your mouth than there are people in the world.

- The average person produces enough saliva in their lifetime to fill two swimming pools.

- The bare space between the eyebrows is called the "glabella"…

- … while the small indentation at the base of the neck between the collar bones is called the "suprasternal notch."

- Around one in every 2,000 babies is born with a tooth already in their mouth.

- Your nose can discern around 50,000 different smells and scents…

- … while your eyes can discern around one million different colors.

- There are 60,000 miles of blood vessels in the human body.

- You sneeze at around 100 mph.

- It takes one red blood cell around 20 seconds to circle around your entire body.

THE HUMAN BODY - POP QUIZ

1. What is the medical name for the tailbone, which because of its resemblance to a curved bird's beak takes its name from the Latin word for "cuckoo"?

2. Human hair, finger and toenails are all made from the same tough protein. What is its name?

3. The hardest substance in the human body isn't bone. What is it?

4. Around one in 200 people have an extra so-called "cervical" rib. How many pairs of ribs do the other 199 people typically have?

5. True or False? Humans can live perfectly well without a spleen.

6. What involuntary bodily movement - which you do roughly 16 times a minute - is properly known as a "blepharospasm"?

7. Your hallux bears around 40% of your body weight when you stand up. How is it better known?

8. How many times does your heart beat a day?
   a. 1,000
   b. 10,000
   c. 100,000
   d. 1,000,000

THE HUMAN BODY - POP QUIZ - SOLUTIONS

1. Coccyx. The coccyx is the lowest and final part of the spinal column.

2. Keratin. It is also the fibrous protein that makes up many creature's hooves, scales, and horns - including the rhinoceros!

3. Tooth enamel. Enamel is also the most mineral-rich substance in the body, with more than 95% of its mass comprised of mineral material.

4. 12. Cervical ribs are a relatively common genetic abnormality, arising in the top of the chest.

5. True. The surgical removal of the spleen is called a splenectomy. Although it is a major part of the body's immune system and is utilized in filtering the blood, you can live healthily without it.

6. Blink. The act of blinking itself is also known as "nictitation."

7. Big toe. In medieval English, the big toe was also known as the "thumb-toe," because of its resemblance to the thumb of the hand.

8. C. 100,000. A normal resting heart rate for adults ranges anywhere from 60 to 100 beats per minute, depending on the age and health of the individual.

27. ENGINEERING WONDERS

- The world's first underground train network was the London Underground. It opened in 1863.

- Despite its name, however, more of the London Underground rail network actually lies above ground, not below it!

- The world's tallest building is the Burj Khalifa. It stands 2,717 feet tall - or just over half a mile!

- The world's first skyscraper was The Home Life Insurance Building, built in Chicago in 1885...

- ... compared to modern skyscrapers though, it wasn't particularly grand and only stood ten stories high, at a height of 138 feet...

- ... and it was pulled down in 1931 - the same year the Empire State Building was completed!

- Of the 100 tallest buildings in the world, the Empire State Building is the oldest.

- The world's tallest completely unoccupied building is thought to be a hotel complex in Pyongyang, the capital of North Korea.

- After its completion in 1884, the 555-foot-tall Washington Monument was the world's tallest humanmade structure...

- ... before then, the world's tallest building was Cologne Cathedral in Germany.

- Completed in 1998, the Petronas Towers in Kuala Lumpur, Malaysia, are the tallest buildings constructed in the 20th century.

- One World Trade Center in New York has 73 elevators.

- The Washington Monument only held the world record for five years, as it was overtaken by the Eiffel Tower in 1889!

○ Incredibly, the Eiffel Tower was originally intended to be only a temporary exhibition as part of the 1889 World's Fair and was meant to be dismantled when the fair was over.

○ The Eiffel Tower is the same height as an 81-story building...

○ ... and is constructed from 10,000 tons of metal held together by 2.5 million rivets!

○ The 1915 Çanakkale Bridge in Turkey - which spans the entire Dardanelles strait - is the longest span of any suspension bridge, longer even than the 1.7-mile Golden Gate Bridge in San Francisco. At its longest, the 1915 has a span of 6,637 feet!

○ Hon Thom Phu Quoc Cable Car in Vietnam is the longest cable car in the world. From start to finish the journey covers almost five miles.

○ Ulm Minister in Germany is the world's tallest ecclesiastical building. It stands 530 feet tall - which is even more extraordinary given that it was completed in 1890!

○ Designed by the famous Spanish architect Antoni Gaudi, The Sagrada Familia church in Barcelona has been under constant construction since 1882.

○ Although the Sagrada Familia has already been consecrated - by Pope Benedict XVI in 2010 - it is not due to be completed until 2026!

○ The design of the Sydney Opera House was open to a public contest. The winning design was made by a Danish architect named Jørn Utzon.

○ Despite their light and graceful appearance, the white sails or "shells" of the Opera House are actually made of white reinforced concrete!

- Sydney Harbour Bridge - or rather the steel posts and main structure used to build it - was constructed 10,000 miles away at a steelworks in Middlesbrough, a town on the east coast of England.

- The world's tallest statue is a gigantic 790-feet-tall effigy of the Indian statesman and independence activist Sardar Vallabhbhai Patel, known as the Statue of Unity. It was officially inaugurated by the Prime Minister of India, Narendra Modi, in 2018.

- The Statue of Liberty's full official name is Liberty Enlightening the World.

- There are 25 windows in the Statue of Liberty's crown.

ENGINEERING WONDERS - POP QUIZ

1. Why is the Eiffel Tower taller on some days rather than others?

2. The Statue of Liberty was famously a gift to America from what European country?

3. True or False? Before the rest of the statue arrived from Europe, the decapitated head of the Statue of Liberty was put on display on its own.

4. What is the name of the grand bridge over the River Thames in London that splits open, in two raised halves, to allow vessels to pass down the river below?

5. Which of these is the tallest?

   a. Statue of Christ the Redeemer, Rio de Janeiro, Brazil
   b. Statue of Liberty, New York, USA
   c. Eiffel Tower, Paris, France
   d. Angel of the North, Gateshead, UK

6. The Hagia Sophia was for a time the world's largest religious building. In what city is it located…?

7. …. and what kind of building is it?

8. The cornerstone ceremony of the Washington Monument took place in 1848. Incredibly, it was attended by three former US presidents, plus the current president at the time. Who was he?

ENGINEERING WONDERS - POP QUIZ - SOLUTIONS

1. Its metal structure swells in hot weather, pushing its height higher!

2. France. The Statue of Liberty was designed by the famous French sculptor Frédéric Auguste Bartholdi - while the metal framework that holds it up was built by Gustave Eiffel, who also made the Eiffel Tower!

3. True! It was put on display partly as a fundraising operation to raise money to complete the work.

4. Tower Bridge. In engineering and architectural terms, Tower Bridge is an example of a so-called double-leaf bascule bridge.

5. C. Eiffel Tower. By some distance, too - at 1,083 feet, it is three times the height of the next tallest on that list, the Statue of Liberty.

6. Istanbul…

7. … Mosque. At the time of its completion in the 6th century, the Hagia Sophia was also the largest enclosed space of any architectural structure yet built.

8. James K Polk. The other three presidents in attendance were James Buchanan, Abraham Lincoln, and Andrew Johnson.

28. MATH & NUMBERS

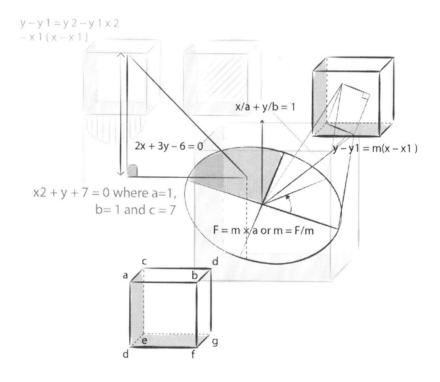

$y - y1 = y2 - y1 x2 - x1(x - x1)$

$x/a + y/b = 1$

$2x + 3y - 6 = 0$

$y - y1 = m(x - x1)$

$x2 + y + 7 = 0$ where a=1, b= 1 and c = 7

$F = m \times a$ or $m = F/m$

○ The individual digits of all multiples of 3 - no matter how great - always total another multiple of 3. So, 27 is a multiple of 3, because $2 + 7 = 9$.

○ Similarly, the total of the digits in any number multiplied by nine will forever reduce down to 9.

○ After a million, a billion, and a trillion comes a quadrillion, a quintillion, a sextillion, a septillion, an octillion, a nonillion, a decillion, and an undecillion!

○ Because all higher numbers in the standard English counting system either end in "–illion" or must have "thousand" or "hundred" in them, every single number name after 88 must contain a letter N.

○ $12,345,679 \times 8 = 98,765,432 \ldots$

○ … while $12,345,679 \times 72 = 888,888,888$!

○ A 1 followed by 100 zeroes is called a googol…

○ … while a 1 followed by a googol of zeroes is called a googolplex!

○ The 762nd, 763rd, 764th, 765th, 766th, and 767th decimal places of pi form a string of consecutive 9s…

○ … the string is known as the Feynman Point, in honor of the famous mathematician Richard Feynman.

○ While $1^2 = 1$, $11^2 = 121$, $111^2 = 12,321$, $1,111^2 = 1,234,321$, and so on!

○ A number that can be expressed as the sum of two cube numbers in two or more different ways is called a taxicab number. The name refers to the number 1729, which was the number of a London taxicab once ridden in by a mathematician named Srinivasa Ramanujan. He later commented on how interesting the number was because 1729 is equal to both $1^3 + 12^3$, and $9^3 + 10^3$!

○ 12,345,679 x 9 = 111,111,111

○ A shape with 100 sides is called a hectogon…

○ … while a shape with 1,000 sides is called a chiliagon.

○ Unless it was particularly large, however, a chiliagon would be barely discernible to the human eye from a circle, as there would have to be almost 3 "sides" inside every degree of an equivalently sized circle.

○ A digit made of repeated numbers, like 11 or 5,555, is called a repdigit.

○ There is no Roman numeral for zero.

○ Opposite numbers on a six-sided die will always add up to 7.

○ In English, every single odd number has an E in its name.

○ 111,111,111 x 111,111,111 = 12,345,678,987,654,321

○ 37 is the 12th prime number, and 73 is the 21st prime number - while 21 is the product of 7 x 3!

○ As a way of quantifying how different larger numbers are, think of this: one million seconds would last around 12 days - but one billion seconds would last 31 years!

○ If you were to put a penny on the first square of a chessboard, then 2 cents on the next square, 4 on the next, then 8, 16, 32, and so on, the final square of the chessboard would have 18 quadrillion dollars on it!

○ 123,456,789 doubled is 246,913,578 - the same nine digits, just in a different order!

○ A number that is the sum of its divisors is called a perfect number….

○ … which makes the smallest perfect number 6, because it is equal to 1 + 2 + 3. The next three are 28, 496, and 8,128.

MATH & NUMBERS - POP QUIZ

1. Incredibly, there are 6,670,903,752,021,072,936,960 possible solvable games of what Japanese number-placing puzzle?

2. What is the smallest and only even prime number?

3. In standard English, what is the smallest number with a three-syllable name?

4. A pronic number is a number that is the product of two consecutive digits, like 12 (which is equal to 3 x 4). What is the next pronic number after that?

5. If a dozen is 12, how many are there in a baker's dozen?

6. The smallest number that can be written as the sum of two prime numbers in two different ways is 10. Name either one of those two ways.

7. What do the words LIVID, MIX, CIVIC, and CIVIL all have in common?

8. Twin primes are a pair of prime numbers that are two digits apart - like 3 and 5 or 5 and 7. So with that definition in mind, what are the two lowest two-digit twin primes?

MATH & NUMBERS - POP QUIZ - SOLUTIONS

1. Sudoku. That's 6.6 sextillion!

2. 2. By definition, a prime number must have two distinct divisors - itself, and 1. Because 1 itself is its own divisor, it does not count as a prime number and so the lowest prime is actually the next number, 2.

3. 11. The smallest number with a four-syllable name, meanwhile, is 27.

4. 20 - which is equal to 4 x 5!

5. 13. A banker's dozen, meanwhile, is 11, while a fisherman's dozen is 20!

6. You can have either 3 + 7, or 5 + 5.

7. They are made from letters that can be used as Roman numerals. The only one of those words that actually works as a Roman numeral, however, is MIX (1,009).

8. 11 and 13. After that, the next twins are 17 and 19.

29. THE SCIENCES

- In Einstein's famous equation e = mc², c represents the speed of light because it is a constant…

- …while e represents energy, and m equals mass!

- The faster you travel; the slower time goes.

- 50% of the world's oxygen is produced by the sea.

- Lightning strikes produce ozone.

- The only two metallic elements that are not silver in color are copper and gold.

- Glass is actually a liquid - it just flows extremely slowly. That's why panes of glass in ancient buildings are sometimes ever so slightly thicker at the bottom than at the top!

- Only two chemical elements are liquid at standard room temperature - mercury and bromine…

- … although a handful of others melt and become liquid just above or below room temperature. The metal gallium, for instance, can be melted in a person's hand!

- The only point at which the Celsius and Fahrenheit temperature scales read the same is –40°.

- The transition of a solid material into a gas without melting and becoming a liquid in between is called sublimation.

- Liquid nitrogen is -196°C (-320°F).

- Dry ice - the strange material used to produce a smoke-like special effect on stage and screen - is actually made of solid carbon dioxide.

- The "triple point" is the point at which a substance can exist in all three basic states of matter - solid, liquid, and gas.

- The triple point of water is 0°C (or rather, just above it) (32°F) as water can be both ice and liquid at this temperature - and, using a vacuum, can be made to boil at its freezing point too!

- The burning filament inside a lightbulb is made of tungsten.

- Tin has the shortest name of all the elements on the periodic table.

- The bizarre effect that causes you to feel pulled forward as a large vehicle speeds past you while waiting at a crossing is called the "Bernoulli effect."

- Because the Earth's plates are constantly moving, Hawaii is gradually drifting toward Alaska, and the Himalayas are growing as India is pushed deeper into mainland Asia!

- It takes eight minutes for light from the sun to reach Earth...

- ... so, if the sun were suddenly to go out, we wouldn't know for several minutes!

- 73% of all the mass of the visible universe is in the form of hydrogen...

- ... which was the very first element created after the Big Bang.

- Theoretically, time travel is possible - but we would only be able to travel forward in time.

- When you add salt to water, the volume of the water decreases slightly.

- Diamond is the hardest material on the planet...

- ... yet like the graphite center of a pencil, it is made of nothing more than pure carbon!

THE SCIENCES - POP QUIZ

1. The rarest naturally occurring element in the Earth's crust has the symbol At. What is its name?

2. DNA forms a strong interlocking shape comprised of a pair of connected spirals called... what?

3. And speaking of DNA, it stands for deoxyribonucleic... what?

4. True or False? Mars appears red to us because of the same chemical that appears when metal rusts.

5. What is the only known non-metallic substance that expands when it freezes?

6. The most expensive element in the world isn't gold but is popularly said to be element number 98 on the period table, with the symbol Cf. What is its name?

7. Which early pioneer of radioactivity was the first woman to win a Nobel Prize, and the first person to win two Nobel Prizes?

8. Approximately how far does light travel in a single second?
   a. 186 miles
   b. 1,860 miles
   c. 18,600 miles
   d. 186,000 miles

THE SCIENCES - POP QUIZ - SOLUTIONS

1. Astatine. Element number 85, astatine's rarity is due to it occurring naturally only as the decay product of heavier elements. The commonest elements in the Earth's crust are oxygen (which makes up more than two-fifths of it), followed by silicon, aluminum, and iron.

2. Double helix. The structure of DNA was first described in 1953.

3. Acid. In chemical terms, DNA is a biopolymer.

4. True! It comprises iron oxide.

5. Water. Water expands by almost 10% when it reaches freezing point.

6. Californium. It is so expensive because it can only be produced in nuclear reactors and particle accelerators.

7. Marie Curie. Madame Curie also remains the only person in history to win a Nobel Prize in two different sciences - physics (1903) and chemistry (1911).

8. D. 186,000 miles. The speed of light is exactly 186,000 miles per second. (Or, put another way, 671 million mph!)

POTLUCK

30. POTLUCK

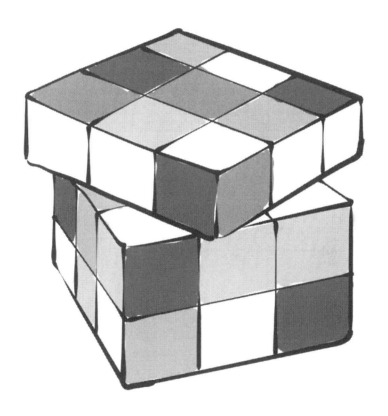

- A Rubik's cube has 43 quintillion different combinations.

- There are 177,147 ways to tie a tie.

- Dolly Parton is Miley Cyrus' godmother.

- The US Flag Act states that any changes to the flag - including new stars added to honor new states joining the Union - can only come into operation on July 4...

- ... but so many states joined the Union in 1817–18, that the following summer the US flag jumped straight from 38 to 43 stars, with no other iterations in between!

- A first wedding anniversary is traditionally a paper anniversary.

- One-third of an inch is called a "barleycorn."

- One-quarter of the world's supply of hazelnuts is used to make Nutella.

- The Breeches Bible was a 1579 edition of the Bible that described Adam and Eve sewing fig leaves together to make trousers.

- Despite the cold, because snow is comprised of around 90–95% air, it is actually a good insulator.

- Some species of moths never develop mouths and so never eat as adults.

- If you were to uncoil an orchestral tuba, the metal pipe would stretch 12 feet.

- Pound cake is so named because early recipes contained one pound of butter, one pound of eggs, and one pound of sugar.

- The number FOUR is the only digit whose name contains the same number of letters that the figure itself represents.

- Nutmeg is faintly hallucinogenic...

- ... and bananas are faintly radioactive!

- Sunday and Monday are named after the Sun and the Moon.

- After his death, the ashes of Fred Baur, the inventor of the Pringles can, were partly buried in a Pringles can at his request.

- The flag of Paraguay is different on opposite sides.

- Spencer Tracy and Tom Hanks are the only actors in Hollywood history to win back-to-back Best Actor Oscars.

- Hair grows around half an inch every month.

- Americans eat the equivalent of 100 acres of pizza every single day.

- Per square mile of territory, the UK gets more tornadoes than the USA.

- Stretching and yawning as a sign of tiredness is called pandiculation.

- Every day, 200 hairs fall out of your head.

- Bifocal spectacles were invented by Benjamin Franklin.

- Crackers have holes in them to prevent them from bubbling as they cook.

POTLUCK - POP QUIZ

1. Why was Walt Disney presented with seven miniature honorary Oscars alongside a regular statuette at the 1939 Academy Awards?

2. What Spanish-origin ballroom dance is often performed by a man and a woman holding a cape between them to symbolize the drama of a bullfight?

3. The letter J was originally added to the alphabet as an alternative form of what other letter?

   a. H
   b. I
   c. K
   d. L

4. What month of the year is named after the two-headed Roman god of entrances and exits?

5. If a male wallaby is called a "jack," what name is given to a female wallaby?

6. True or False? The Bible is America's most shoplifted book.

7. How long is the world's longest earthworm?

   a. Two feet
   b. Eight feet
   c. 14 ft
   d. 21 ft

8. What does the poison cyanide have in common with marzipan?

POTLUCK - POP QUIZ- SOLUTIONS

1. The awards were to celebrate the groundbreaking success of Snow White and the Seven Dwarfs.

2. Paso doble. The name paso doble literally means "double step" in Spanish.

3. I. In some older dictionaries, in fact, I- and J- words are sometimes listed together!

4. January. The god Janus is said to have looked back on the year now gone, and ahead to the new year simultaneously.

5. Jill. Jack and Jill are also the names given to male and female hares, ferrets, opossums, and weasels.

6. True! The Bible ranks so highly because these figures include data from public libraries, where reference books - including religious texts, dictionaries, encyclopedias, and atlases - are frequently taken out but never returned!

7. D. 21 feet! Named Microchaetus rappi, it lives in southern Africa.

8. Almonds! Marzipan is made of ground almond meal, while cyanide smells faintly of burned almonds.

CONCLUSION

And with that final pop quiz - and with those final extraordinary facts! - Our journey through more than 1,000 bizarre and amazing tidbits of information is complete!

From Hadrian to horses, koalas to kings, and Beethoven to the Bible, we've covered quite a few different topics along the way here - and traveled not just all around the world, from one hemisphere to the other, but to the bottom of the oceans, out through our solar system into space, and far, far beyond!

If you're a true trivia nerd, perhaps you knew one or two of these bizarre facts beforehand. But hopefully, somewhere in these past 30 chapters or so, you'll have learned more than a few new bits and pieces of trivia to keep your brain engaged and - when next you need it - —the conversation flowing.

With that in mind, how about one last fact? Did you know the average person has 27 conversations every day? Now that really is a conversation starter...

Made in the USA
Las Vegas, NV
16 October 2024

97011082R10109